Central Statistics Office

Agricultural Statistics of Ireland

1873

Central Statistics Office

Agricultural Statistics of Ireland
1873

ISBN/EAN: 9783741122194

Manufactured in Europe, USA, Canada, Australia, Japa

Cover: Foto ©Lupo / pixelio.de

Manufactured and distributed by brebook publishing software
(www.brebook.com)

Central Statistics Office

Agricultural Statistics of Ireland

AGRICULTURAL STATISTICS, IRELAND.

TABLES

SHOWING THE

ESTIMATED AVERAGE PRODUCE

OF

THE CROPS

FOR THE YEAR

1873;

AND THE

EMIGRATION FROM IRISH PORTS,
FROM 1st JANUARY TO 31st DECEMBER, 1873;
ALSO THE NUMBER OF MILLS FOR SCUTCHING FLAX
IN EACH COUNTY AND PROVINCE.

Presented to both Houses of Parliament by Command of Her Majesty.

DUBLIN:
PRINTED BY ALEXANDER THOM, 87 & 88, ABBEY-STREET,
FOR HER MAJESTY'S STATIONERY OFFICE.

1874.

[C.—956.] *Price 6½d.*

CONTENTS.

TABLES.

AGRICULTURAL STATISTICS, IRELAND.

THE ESTIMATED AVERAGE PRODUCE OF THE CROPS:

ALSO,

THE EMIGRATION FROM IRELAND

IN THE YEAR 1873,

AND THE

NUMBER OF MILLS FOR SCUTCHING FLAX IN EACH COUNTY AND PROVINCE.

TO HIS GRACE JAMES, DUKE OF ABERCORN, K.G.,

LORD LIEUTENANT-GENERAL AND GENERAL GOVERNOR OF IRELAND,

&c. &c. &c.

MAY IT PLEASE YOUR GRACE,

On the 7th of August, 1873, I had the honour of submitting a Return of the acreage under Flax in 1872 and 1873; on the 11th of the same month a Return giving the number and value of live stock in Ireland from 1861 to 1873 inclusive, and on the 24th of September, General Abstracts, showing, by Counties and Provinces, the extent under the various crops, and the number of live stock in 1872 and 1873, together with an Appendix containing extracts from the works of the late Sir John Sinclair, Professor Buckman, and other eminent writers, as to the great importance of extirpating weeds. I now beg to bring under your Grace's consideration Tables which give the *estimated average produce* of the principal crops, and the total emigration from this country in 1873.

The Tables relating to the *average produce* of the crops per acre, have been carefully compiled, as in former years, from information obtained by members of the Royal Irish Constabulary and Metropolitan Police, from practical farmers, and others conversant with the yield in the *electoral division* for which the Return was made. The names and residences of the various parties affording the information are stated on the forms by the Enumerators. *Mode of collecting the Returns of Produce.*

Copies of these Returns were forwarded by me to the Chairman and Board of Guardians of each Union, for revision, and I have the satisfaction to state, that out of 3,438—the entire number of electoral divisions in Ireland—Returns revised or approved by the Guardians* have been received for 2,487 electoral divisions.

The *area* under crops as published in the "General Abstracts" has been carefully revised, and the figures used in making the present calculations; so that the *average* yield, as given in the following Tables, is as approximately accurate as can be expected in returns of this description.

The acreage under crops in 1873, as compared with 1872, shows a decrease in cereal crops—in wheat of 37,780 acres, oats 118,739 acres, bere and rye 731 acres. Barley increased by 11,102 acres. Potatoes decreased by 68,609 acres—(and yet afforded an increase in yield of 877,333 tons),—and cabbage by 11,337 acres. Turnips show an increase of 1,187 acres, mangel wurzel 3,455 acres, flax 7,803 acres, and hay of 87,975 acres.

The crops which show an increased *estimated average produce* per acre in 1873, compared with 1872, are—wheat 0·3 cwt., oats 1·4 cwt., barley 1·6 cwt., bere 0·2 cwt., rye 0·7 cwt., potatoes 1·2 tons, turnips 1·8 tons, mangel wurzel 1·1 tons, and flax 7·2 stones. Hay shows a decrease of 0·1 ton.

In the *estimated total* produce of cereal crops there is an increase of 263,846 quarters; in oats the increase is 258,308 quarters, in barley 146,794 quarters, and in rye 325 quarters. There is a decrease in wheat of 140,263 quarters, and in bere 1,315 quarters. In green crops—potatoes *increased* by 877,333 tons, turnips by 466,689 tons, mangel wurzel by 64,908 tons, and flax by 2,754 tons. Cabbage *decreased* by 110,011 tons, and hay by 189,553 tons.

The acreage under the principal crops in 1872 and 1873, and the increase or decrease in the latter year, are given in Table I.; the *estimated average produce* per acre and the *total yield* in Tables II. and III.; a comparison of the *average produce* of the crops per acre in each county and province in 1872 and 1873, in Table IV.; and in Table V. *The acreage under Crops, and estimated average*

* Copies of the forms and circulars used in obtaining the information are given at pages 58 and 59.

A 2

produce in 1872 and 1873. the total extent under the principal crops, the total produce, and the *estimated* average yield per acre, for each year from 1851 to 1873, inclusive.

There can be no doubt that if due care was bestowed on the cultivation of the lands of Ireland, the outlay would be amply repaid by a largely increased yield; but, unfortunately, crops of *weeds*, which are to be seen in almost every part of the country, not only rob the farmer himself, but often inflict a vast amount of injury on his neighbour. It has been estimated that the money loss to Ireland from the above cause exceeds *a million and a half*.

TABLE I.—The total acreage under each of the principal Crops in 1872 and 1873, and the increase or decrease in the latter year.

Crops.	Extent Cultivated in		Increase or Decrease in 1873.	
	1872.	1873.	Increase.	Decrease.
	Acres.	Acres.	Acres.	Acres.
Wheat,	226,294	167,554	.	57,740
Oats,	1,624,711	1,510,979	.	113,739
Barley,	219,013	230,118	11,105	.
Bere and Rye,	9,975	9,224	.	751
Potatoes,	991,871	903,263	.	88,609
Turnips,	346,711	347,848	1,137	.
Mangel Wurzel,	34,702	38,157	3,455	.
Cabbage,	39,462	23,118	.	11,357
Flax,	121,997	129,297	7,300	.
Hay,	1,800,573	1,838,143	37,573	.
Net Decrease,			211,570	

TABLE II.—The *estimated average produce* per statute acre of the principal Crops in 1872 and 1873, and the increase or decrease in 1873.

Crops.	Produce per Acre		Increase or Decrease in 1873	
	1872.	1873.	Increase.	Decrease.
Wheat, in Cwts.	11·4	11·7	0·3	.
Oats, "	11·4	12·5	1·1	.
Barley, "	14·3	15·9	1·6	.
Bere, "	14·6	11·8	0·2	.
Rye, "	9·7	10·4	0·7	.
Potatoes, in Tons,	1·8	3·0	1·2	.
Turnips, "	11·4	12·7	1·3	.
Mangel Wurzel, in Tons,	12·4	13·5	1·1	.
Cabbage, in Tons,	9·9	9·9	.	.
Flax, in Stones of 14 lbs.,	27·4	31·4	3·7	.
Hay, in Tons,	1·9	1·8	.	0·1

TABLE III.—The *estimated total* produce of the principal Crops in 1872 and 1873, and the increase or decrease in the latter year.

Crops.	Estimated Produce		Increase or Decrease in 1873.	
	1872.	1873.	Increase.	Decrease.
	Quarters.	Quarters.	Quarters.	Quarters.
Wheat,	629,831	469,563	.	160,268
Oats,	6,631,456	6,918,765	283,309	.
Barley,	865,715	1,010,539	144,791	.
Bere,	6,452	4,959	.	1,513
Rye,	31,115	31,833	718	.
	Tons.	Tons.	Tons.	Tons.
Potatoes,	1,824,837	2,653,060	877,832	.
Turnips,	3,963,308	4,129,967	166,663	.
Mangel Wurzel,	430,752	516,660	84,908	.
Cabbage,	386,934	276,923	.	110,011
Flax,	17,059	19,813	2,754	.
Hay,	3,493,996	3,304,163	.	189,833

TABLE IV.—The *average acreable yield* of the principal Crops in 1877 and 1878, by Counties and Provinces. Acreable yield of the Crops in 1877 and 1878.

Counties and Provinces.	[illegible]	[illegible]	[illegible]	[illegible]	[illegible]	[illegible]	[illegible]	[illegible]	[illegible]	[illegible]	[illegible]
Antrim	[illegible]	[illegible]	[illegible]	[illegible]	[illegible]	[illegible]	[illegible]	[illegible]	[illegible]	[illegible]	[illegible]
Armagh	[illegible]	[illegible]	[illegible]	[illegible]	[illegible]	[illegible]	[illegible]	[illegible]	[illegible]	[illegible]	[illegible]
Carlow	[illegible]	[illegible]	[illegible]	[illegible]	[illegible]	[illegible]	[illegible]	[illegible]	[illegible]	[illegible]	[illegible]
Cavan	[illegible]	[illegible]	[illegible]	[illegible]	[illegible]	[illegible]	[illegible]	[illegible]	[illegible]	[illegible]	[illegible]
Clare	[illegible]	[illegible]	[illegible]	[illegible]	[illegible]	[illegible]	[illegible]	[illegible]	[illegible]	[illegible]	[illegible]
Cork	[illegible]	[illegible]	[illegible]	[illegible]	[illegible]	[illegible]	[illegible]	[illegible]	[illegible]	[illegible]	[illegible]
Donegal	[illegible]	[illegible]	[illegible]	[illegible]	[illegible]	[illegible]	[illegible]	[illegible]	[illegible]	[illegible]	[illegible]
Down	[illegible]	[illegible]	[illegible]	[illegible]	[illegible]	[illegible]	[illegible]	[illegible]	[illegible]	[illegible]	[illegible]
Dublin	[illegible]	[illegible]	[illegible]	[illegible]	[illegible]	[illegible]	[illegible]	[illegible]	[illegible]	[illegible]	[illegible]
Fermanagh	[illegible]	[illegible]	[illegible]	[illegible]	[illegible]	[illegible]	[illegible]	[illegible]	[illegible]	[illegible]	[illegible]
Galway	[illegible]	[illegible]	[illegible]	[illegible]	[illegible]	[illegible]	[illegible]	[illegible]	[illegible]	[illegible]	[illegible]
Kerry	[illegible]	[illegible]	[illegible]	[illegible]	[illegible]	[illegible]	[illegible]	[illegible]	[illegible]	[illegible]	[illegible]
Kildare	[illegible]	[illegible]	[illegible]	[illegible]	[illegible]	[illegible]	[illegible]	[illegible]	[illegible]	[illegible]	[illegible]
Kilkenny	[illegible]	[illegible]	[illegible]	[illegible]	[illegible]	[illegible]	[illegible]	[illegible]	[illegible]	[illegible]	[illegible]
King's	[illegible]	[illegible]	[illegible]	[illegible]	[illegible]	[illegible]	[illegible]	[illegible]	[illegible]	[illegible]	[illegible]
Leitrim	[illegible]	[illegible]	[illegible]	[illegible]	[illegible]	[illegible]	[illegible]	[illegible]	[illegible]	[illegible]	[illegible]
Limerick	[illegible]	[illegible]	[illegible]	[illegible]	[illegible]	[illegible]	[illegible]	[illegible]	[illegible]	[illegible]	[illegible]
Londonderry	[illegible]	[illegible]	[illegible]	[illegible]	[illegible]	[illegible]	[illegible]	[illegible]	[illegible]	[illegible]	[illegible]
Longford	[illegible]	[illegible]	[illegible]	[illegible]	[illegible]	[illegible]	[illegible]	[illegible]	[illegible]	[illegible]	[illegible]
Louth	[illegible]	[illegible]	[illegible]	[illegible]	[illegible]	[illegible]	[illegible]	[illegible]	[illegible]	[illegible]	[illegible]
Mayo	[illegible]	[illegible]	[illegible]	[illegible]	[illegible]	[illegible]	[illegible]	[illegible]	[illegible]	[illegible]	[illegible]
Meath	[illegible]	[illegible]	[illegible]	[illegible]	[illegible]	[illegible]	[illegible]	[illegible]	[illegible]	[illegible]	[illegible]
Monaghan	[illegible]	[illegible]	[illegible]	[illegible]	[illegible]	[illegible]	[illegible]	[illegible]	[illegible]	[illegible]	[illegible]
Queen's	[illegible]	[illegible]	[illegible]	[illegible]	[illegible]	[illegible]	[illegible]	[illegible]	[illegible]	[illegible]	[illegible]
Roscommon	[illegible]	[illegible]	[illegible]	[illegible]	[illegible]	[illegible]	[illegible]	[illegible]	[illegible]	[illegible]	[illegible]
Sligo	[illegible]	[illegible]	[illegible]	[illegible]	[illegible]	[illegible]	[illegible]	[illegible]	[illegible]	[illegible]	[illegible]
Tipperary	[illegible]	[illegible]	[illegible]	[illegible]	[illegible]	[illegible]	[illegible]	[illegible]	[illegible]	[illegible]	[illegible]
Tyrone	[illegible]	[illegible]	[illegible]	[illegible]	[illegible]	[illegible]	[illegible]	[illegible]	[illegible]	[illegible]	[illegible]
Waterford	[illegible]	[illegible]	[illegible]	[illegible]	[illegible]	[illegible]	[illegible]	[illegible]	[illegible]	[illegible]	[illegible]
Westmeath	[illegible]	[illegible]	[illegible]	[illegible]	[illegible]	[illegible]	[illegible]	[illegible]	[illegible]	[illegible]	[illegible]
Wexford	[illegible]	[illegible]	[illegible]	[illegible]	[illegible]	[illegible]	[illegible]	[illegible]	[illegible]	[illegible]	[illegible]
Wicklow	[illegible]	[illegible]	[illegible]	[illegible]	[illegible]	[illegible]	[illegible]	[illegible]	[illegible]	[illegible]	[illegible]

EXTENT UNDER CROPS IN STATUTE MEASURE.

Years	Wheat	Oats	Barley	Bere	Rye	Potatoes	Turnips	Mangel Wurzel	Cabbage	Flax	Hay
	Acres	Acres	Acres	Acres	Acres	Acres	Acres	Acres	Acres	Acres	Acres
[illegible]	[illegible]	[illegible]	[illegible]	[illegible]	[illegible]	[illegible]	[illegible]	[illegible]	[illegible]	[illegible]	[illegible]

ESTIMATED TOTAL PRODUCE.

Years	Wheat	Oats	Barley	Bere	Rye	Potatoes	Turnips	Mangel Wurzel	Cabbage	Flax	Hay
	Quarters	Quarters	Quarters	Quarters	Quarters	Tons	Tons	Tons	Tons	Tons	Tons
[illegible]	[illegible]	[illegible]	[illegible]	[illegible]	[illegible]	[illegible]	[illegible]	[illegible]	[illegible]	[illegible]	[illegible]

ESTIMATED AVERAGE PRODUCE PER STATUTE ACRE.

Years	Wheat	Oats	Barley	Bere	Rye	Potatoes	Turnips	Mangel Wurzel	Cabbage	Flax	Hay
[illegible]	[illegible]	[illegible]	[illegible]	[illegible]	[illegible]	[illegible]	[illegible]	[illegible]	[illegible]	[illegible]	[illegible]

METEOROLOGICAL OBSERVATIONS.

Meteorological Observations.

In connexion with the Agricultural Statistics, I beg to give the following abstract (Table VI.) of the Meteorological Observations registered at the Ordnance Survey Office, in the Phœnix Park, during the year 1873, for which I am indebted to the courtesy of Colonel Wilkinson, R.E.

The barometer stood highest in 1873 on the 21st of February, at 9.30 A.M.,—wind calm—when it was 30·744 inches; it was lowest at 9.30 P.M. on the 20th of January,—wind calm—when it was 28·470 inches. The highest temperature of the air during the year was 81·6 degrees of Fahrenheit, on July 20th, and the lowest 23·0 degrees, on February 2nd, November 2nd, and December 11th. The greatest quantity of rain which fell in a day (24 hours) was 1·280 inches, on the 18th of September—the wind being W. The point from which the wind chiefly prevailed was the W.; it blew from that direction 69 days, with an average pressure of 3·47 lbs. per square foot. The strongest wind was from the S.W., on the 21st of December, when the pressure was 25 lbs. per square foot.

TABLE VI.—METEOROLOGICAL OBSERVATIONS taken at the Ordnance Survey Office, Phœnix Park, Dublin, in 1873. Height above the sea, 156·8 feet.

1873.	[illegible] Thermometers				Hygrometer					Rain Gauge			Cloud		
	[illegible]	[illegible]	[illegible]	[illegible]	[illegible]	[illegible]	[illegible]	[illegible]	[illegible]	[illegible]	[illegible]	[illegible]	[illegible]	[illegible]	[illegible]
January,	[illegible]	[illegible]	[illegible]	[illegible]	[illegible]	[illegible]	[illegible]	[illegible]	[illegible]	[illegible]	[illegible]	[illegible]	[illegible]	[illegible]	[illegible]
February,	[illegible]	[illegible]	[illegible]	[illegible]	[illegible]	[illegible]	[illegible]	[illegible]	[illegible]	[illegible]	[illegible]	[illegible]	[illegible]	[illegible]	[illegible]
March,	[illegible]	[illegible]	[illegible]	[illegible]	[illegible]	[illegible]	[illegible]	[illegible]	[illegible]	[illegible]	[illegible]	[illegible]	[illegible]	[illegible]	[illegible]
April,	[illegible]	[illegible]	[illegible]	[illegible]	[illegible]	[illegible]	[illegible]	[illegible]	[illegible]	[illegible]	[illegible]	[illegible]	[illegible]	[illegible]	[illegible]
May,	[illegible]	[illegible]	[illegible]	[illegible]	[illegible]	[illegible]	[illegible]	[illegible]	[illegible]	[illegible]	[illegible]	[illegible]	[illegible]	[illegible]	[illegible]
June,	[illegible]	[illegible]	[illegible]	[illegible]	[illegible]	[illegible]	[illegible]	[illegible]	[illegible]	[illegible]	[illegible]	[illegible]	[illegible]	[illegible]	[illegible]
July,	[illegible]	[illegible]	[illegible]	[illegible]	[illegible]	[illegible]	[illegible]	[illegible]	[illegible]	[illegible]	[illegible]	[illegible]	[illegible]	[illegible]	[illegible]
August,	[illegible]	[illegible]	[illegible]	[illegible]	[illegible]	[illegible]	[illegible]	[illegible]	[illegible]	[illegible]	[illegible]	[illegible]	[illegible]	[illegible]	[illegible]
September,	[illegible]	[illegible]	[illegible]	[illegible]	[illegible]	[illegible]	[illegible]	[illegible]	[illegible]	[illegible]	[illegible]	[illegible]	[illegible]	[illegible]	[illegible]
October,	[illegible]	[illegible]	[illegible]	[illegible]	[illegible]	[illegible]	[illegible]	[illegible]	[illegible]	[illegible]	[illegible]	[illegible]	[illegible]	[illegible]	[illegible]
November,	[illegible]	[illegible]	[illegible]	[illegible]	[illegible]	[illegible]	[illegible]	[illegible]	[illegible]	[illegible]	[illegible]	[illegible]	[illegible]	[illegible]	[illegible]
December,	[illegible]	[illegible]	[illegible]	[illegible]	[illegible]	[illegible]	[illegible]	[illegible]	[illegible]	[illegible]	[illegible]	[illegible]	[illegible]	[illegible]	[illegible]
Total,	[illegible]	[illegible]	[illegible]	.	[illegible]	[illegible]	[illegible]	[illegible]	[illegible]	[illegible]	[illegible]	.	[illegible]	[illegible]	[illegible]
Mean,	[illegible]	[illegible]	[illegible]	.	[illegible]	[illegible]	[illegible]	[illegible]	[illegible]	.	.	.	.	.	.

1873.	Barometer				Wind								
	[illegible]	[illegible]	[illegible]	[illegible]	N.	N.E.	E.	S.E.	S.	S.W.	W.	N.W.	Calm
January,	[illegible]	[illegible]	[illegible]	[illegible]	[illegible]	[illegible]	[illegible]	[illegible]	[illegible]	[illegible]	[illegible]	[illegible]	[illegible]
February,	[illegible]	[illegible]	[illegible]	[illegible]	[illegible]	[illegible]	[illegible]	[illegible]	[illegible]	[illegible]	[illegible]	[illegible]	[illegible]
March,	[illegible]	[illegible]	[illegible]	[illegible]	[illegible]	[illegible]	[illegible]	[illegible]	[illegible]	[illegible]	[illegible]	[illegible]	[illegible]
April,	[illegible]	[illegible]	[illegible]	[illegible]	[illegible]	[illegible]	[illegible]	[illegible]	[illegible]	[illegible]	[illegible]	[illegible]	[illegible]
May,	[illegible]	[illegible]	[illegible]	[illegible]	[illegible]	[illegible]	[illegible]	[illegible]	[illegible]	[illegible]	[illegible]	[illegible]	[illegible]
June,	[illegible]	[illegible]	[illegible]	[illegible]	[illegible]	[illegible]	[illegible]	[illegible]	[illegible]	[illegible]	[illegible]	[illegible]	[illegible]
July,	[illegible]	[illegible]	[illegible]	[illegible]	[illegible]	[illegible]	[illegible]	[illegible]	[illegible]	[illegible]	[illegible]	[illegible]	[illegible]
August,	[illegible]	[illegible]	[illegible]	[illegible]	[illegible]	[illegible]	[illegible]	[illegible]	[illegible]	[illegible]	[illegible]	[illegible]	[illegible]
September,	[illegible]	[illegible]	[illegible]	[illegible]	[illegible]	[illegible]	[illegible]	[illegible]	[illegible]	[illegible]	[illegible]	[illegible]	[illegible]
October,	[illegible]	[illegible]	[illegible]	[illegible]	[illegible]	[illegible]	[illegible]	[illegible]	[illegible]	[illegible]	[illegible]	[illegible]	[illegible]
November,	[illegible]	[illegible]	[illegible]	[illegible]	[illegible]	[illegible]	[illegible]	[illegible]	[illegible]	[illegible]	[illegible]	[illegible]	[illegible]
December,	[illegible]	[illegible]	[illegible]	[illegible]	[illegible]	[illegible]	[illegible]	[illegible]	[illegible]	[illegible]	[illegible]	[illegible]	[illegible]
Total,	[illegible]	[illegible]	[illegible]	.	[illegible]	[illegible]	[illegible]	[illegible]	[illegible]	[illegible]	[illegible]	[illegible]	[illegible]
Mean,	[illegible]	[illegible]	[illegible]	.	.	.	.	.	.	.	.	.	.

EMIGRATION FROM IRISH PORTS IN 1873.

Emigration from Irish Ports.

The number of emigrants who left the Irish ports in 1873 was 90,992, being an increase of 12,211 compared with 1872.

The number of *males* who emigrated in 1873 was 52,376, being 5,835 more than in the previous year; the *females* amounted to 38,616, being an increase of 6,376, compared with 1872.

Emigration from Irish Ports.

The following Table (VII.) gives the number from each Province in 1872 and 1873, distinguishing the sexes.

TABLE VII.—The Emigration from each Province during 1872 and 1873.

Emigrated from	Males		Females		Total	
	1872.	1873.	1872.	1873.	1872.	1873.
Provinces: Leinster,	10,127	9,729	8,164	8,462	18,291	18,191
Munster,	8,719	11,971	8,[illegible]	10,128	16,[illegible]	22,109
Ulster,	22,072	21,[illegible]	12,660	12,065	34,732	33,[illegible]
Connaught,	5,[illegible]	8,[illegible]	4,453	7,471	9,[illegible]	15,[illegible]
From what Province not stated,	88	63	[illegible]	43	111	106
Persons belonging to other Countries,	[illegible]	646	160	197	879	843
Total,	48,741	52,276	23,040	28,416	71,781	80,992
Increase in 1873,	5,535		5,374		12,211	

The succeeding Table is in continuation of one published annually for some years past, and gives the number and sex of the Emigrants from each County and Province, since the 1st of May, 1851—(the date at which the collection of these Returns at the several Irish Ports was commenced)—to the 31st of December, 1873; also the proportion per cent. for each County and Province on the total number of Emigrants who left Ireland during that period.

TABLE VIII.—Table showing by Counties and Provinces the Number of Emigrants (distinguishing Males and Females) who left Ireland from 1st May, 1851, to 31st December, 1873, and the per-centage from each County.

Number.	Provinces and Counties.	Number of Emigrants from 1st May, 1851, to 31st December, 1873. Males.	Females.	Total.	Proportion per cent. of Emigrants from each County to the total Emigration.	Number.
	LEINSTER.					
1	Carlow,	9,612	9,037	18,[illegible]	0·[illegible]	1
2	Dublin, and City,	35,402	29,091	64,495	2·83	2
3	Kildare,	12,164	10,240	22,404	0·98	3
4	Kilkenny, and City,	25,681	24,002	49,683	2·15	4
5	King's,	19,134	16,187	37,271	1·61	5
6	Longford,	17,829	15,765	33,094	1·48	6
7	Louth, and Drogheda,	14,614	15,740	30,354	1·35	7
8	Meath,	23,571	21,154	44,725	1·96	8
9	Queen's,	17,343	16,328	33,671	1·47	9
10	Westmeath,	17,145	15,333	32,798	1·44	10
11	Wexford,	26,283	23,095	49,378	2·15	11
12	Wicklow,	10,131	8,512	18,643	0·82	12
	TOTAL,	248,581	207,076	455,657	19·11	
	MUNSTER.					
13	Clare,	43,054	43,325	86,379	3·79	13
14	Cork, and City,	147,391	133,833	281,724	12·30	14
15	Kerry,	52,751	43,893	107,444	4·30	15
16	Limerick, and City,	59,132	56,979	116,112	4·95	16
17	Tipperary,	71,794	66,637	138,431	6·06	17
18	Waterford, and City,	34,916	27,955	62,844	2·76	18
	TOTAL,	405,533	375,599	787,138	34·64	

TABLE VIII.—*continued*.

Emigration from Irish Ports.

Number.	Provinces and Counties.	Number of Emigrants from 1st May, 1851, to 31st December, 1873. Males.	Females.	Total.	Proportion per cent. of Emigrants from each County to the total Emigration.	Number.
	ULSTER.					
19	Antrim,	92,463	63,313	155,876	6·83	19
20	Armagh,	31,813	33,081	64,897	2·41	20
21	Cavan,	34,486	31,991	65,477	2·91	21
22	Donegal,	32,748	27,906	60,654	1·96	22
23	Down,	45,063	34,385	68,447	3·82	23
24	Fermanagh,	16,413	16,716	33,129	1·41	24
25	Londonderry,	30,138	23,070	53,168	2·33	25
26	Monaghan,	23,770	23,034	47,804	2·10	26
27	Tyrone,	41,390	33,316	74,744	3·28	27
	TOTAL,	360,143	271,877	632,014	27·56	.
	CONNAUGHT.					
28	Galway, and Town,	50,297	46,060	96,357	4·21	28
29	Leitrim,	18,311	17,329	35,110	1·56	29
30	Mayo,	33,663	32,789	66,396	2·91	30
31	Roscommon,	28,320	26,444	54,764	2·40	31
32	Sligo,	14,704	15,111	29,816	1·31	32
	TOTAL,	144,943	138,643	284,603	12·49	.
33	*From what County not specified*,	61,693	48,898	110,591	4·85	33
34	*Persons belonging to other Countries who embarked at Irish Ports from 1853 to* 1873, *inclusive*,	17,945	8,411	26,356	1·15	34
	TOTAL,	1,321,944	1,057,157	2,379,101	.	.

The ages of the emigrants are given by provinces, in Table IX., from which it appears that in 1873—76·7 in every 100 of the persons who left Ireland were between the ages of 15 and 35 years. In 1872 the proportion per cent. for those ages was 77·6 per cent.

TABLE IX.—NUMBERS and AGES of EMIGRANTS from each Province, and from all Ireland during 1873:—

Ages.	Leinster. Number of Persons.	Leinster. Proportion per cent. of each age-period.	Munster. Number of Persons.	Munster. Proportion per cent. of each age-period.	Ulster. Number of Persons.	Ulster. Proportion per cent. of each age-period.	Connaught. Number of Persons.	Connaught. Proportion per cent. of each age-period.	From what Province not specified. No. of Persons.	Belonging to other Countries. No. of Persons.	General Total. Number of Persons.	General Total. Proportion per cent. of each age-period.
Under 1 year,	105	0·6	54	0·2	223	0·6	48	0·3	.	5	401	0·4
1 and under 5,	780	4·9	1,332	5·7	1,087	3·3	637	4·0	6	33	3,794	4·2
5 " 15,	1,309	8·3	2,106	9·5	2,576	7·8	1,438	9·1	3	76	7,503	8·3
15 " 25,	9,165	50·5	11,019	50·0	14,183	43·6	8,707	55·1	56	243	44,163	50·3
25 " 35,	3,729	23·0	5,579	25·5	11,502	34·7	3,151	22·0	28	355	24,829	26·3
35 " 45,	1,106	6·1	1,347	5·6	2,003	7·7	379	3·0	7	121	5,863	6·4
45 " 55,	366	2·2	334	2·6	770	2·6	197	2·2	5	33	2,071	2·6
55 " 65,	143	0·9	163	0·7	311	0·9	115	0·8	1	6	730	0·8
65 and upwards,	25	0·1	6	.	34	0·1	13	0·1	.	.	78	0·1
Age not specified,	1	.	4	.	1	.	4	.	.	.	10	.
Total,	18,191	100·	22,159	100·	33,067	100·	14,786	100·	106	873	90,077	100·

SCUTCHING MILLS IN IRELAND.

A Table is given commencing at page 25, showing by Provinces, Counties, Baronies, Parishes and Townlands, the locality of every Mill for scutching Flax; the number of Stocks and Handles in each; and the period, in weeks, during which every Mill was at work, from the 1st of June, 1872, to the 31st of May, 1873. There were 1,437 of these Mills at the time the Statistics were collected, (in June, 1873,) of which 1,335 were in Ulster,—29 in Leinster,—33 in Munster,—and 30 in Connaught.

The following is the number of these Mills, in each year, from 1864 to 1873, inclusive, by Provinces:—

Provinces.	1864.	1865.	1866.	1867.	1868.	1869.	1870.	1871.	1872.	1873.
1. Ulster,	1,118	1,311	[illegible]	1,418	1,480	[illegible]	1,408	1,381	1,376	1,335
2. Leinster,	18	54	59	83	67	56	39	60	54	29
3. Munster,	13	43	39	43	41	41	38	39	33	23
4. Connaught,	1	24	33	38	34	35	31	33	31	30
Ireland,	[illegible]	[illegible]	[illegible]	[illegible]	[illegible]	[illegible]	[illegible]	[illegible]	[illegible]	[illegible]

I beg to repeat my respectful acknowledgments for the continued assistance afforded to the Enumerators by the landed proprietors and tenant-farmers of Ireland who furnished the particulars from which the foregoing tables have been compiled. I have also to express my best thanks to the several Boards of Guardians by whom the *average acreable yield* of the crops has been revised; and to the Metropolitan and Provincial press for making widely known the importance of these Statistics. It affords me much satisfaction to state to your Grace that those members of the Royal Irish Constabulary and Metropolitan Police who acted as Superintendents of the work, and also the Enumerators discharged this duty with their usual efficiency.

I have the honour to be,
Your Grace's
Very faithful servant,
William Donnelly,
Registrar-General.

General Register Office,
Charlemont House, Dublin,
31st March, 1874.

TABLES

SHOWING THE

ESTIMATED AVERAGE PRODUCE

OF

THE CROPS

FOR THE YEAR

1873.

[illegible]	[illegible]			[illegible]			[illegible]			[illegible]			[illegible]			[illegible]		
	[illegible]	[illegible]	[illegible]	[illegible]	[illegible]	[illegible]	[illegible]	[illegible]	[illegible]	[illegible]	[illegible]	[illegible]	[illegible]	[illegible]	[illegible]	[illegible]	[illegible]	[illegible]
[illegible]	[illegible]	[illegible]	[illegible]	[illegible]	[illegible]	[illegible]	[illegible]	[illegible]	[illegible]	[illegible]	[illegible]	[illegible]	[illegible]	[illegible]	[illegible]	[illegible]	[illegible]	[illegible]

IRELAND, IN 1872 AND 1873; ALSO THE PRODUCE OF POTATOES, IN TONS; THESE YEARS—IN STATUTE MEASURE.

Beans 1872	Beans 1873	Pease 1872	Pease 1873	Estimated Produce of Potatoes 1872	Estimated Produce of Potatoes 1873	Cereal Crops 1872	Cereal Crops 1873	Potatoes 1872	Potatoes 1873	Other Green Crops 1872	Other Green Crops 1873	Meadow and Clover 1872	Meadow and Clover 1873	Provinces and Counties.
														LEINSTER.
[illegible]	[illegible]	[illegible]	[illegible]	[illegible]	[illegible]	[illegible]	[illegible]	[illegible]	[illegible]	[illegible]	[illegible]	[illegible]	[illegible]	Carlow.
[illegible]	[illegible]	[illegible]	[illegible]	[illegible]	[illegible]	[illegible]	[illegible]	[illegible]	[illegible]	[illegible]	[illegible]	[illegible]	[illegible]	Dublin.
[illegible]	[illegible]	[illegible]	[illegible]	[illegible]	[illegible]	[illegible]	[illegible]	[illegible]	[illegible]	[illegible]	[illegible]	[illegible]	[illegible]	Kildare.
[illegible]	[illegible]	[illegible]	[illegible]	[illegible]	[illegible]	[illegible]	[illegible]	[illegible]	[illegible]	[illegible]	[illegible]	[illegible]	[illegible]	Kilkenny.
[illegible]	[illegible]	[illegible]	[illegible]	[illegible]	[illegible]	[illegible]	[illegible]	[illegible]	[illegible]	[illegible]	[illegible]	[illegible]	[illegible]	King's.
[illegible]	[illegible]	[illegible]	[illegible]	[illegible]	[illegible]	[illegible]	[illegible]	[illegible]	[illegible]	[illegible]	[illegible]	[illegible]	[illegible]	Longford.
[illegible]	[illegible]	[illegible]	[illegible]	[illegible]	[illegible]	[illegible]	[illegible]	[illegible]	[illegible]	[illegible]	[illegible]	[illegible]	[illegible]	Louth.
[illegible]	[illegible]	[illegible]	[illegible]	[illegible]	[illegible]	[illegible]	[illegible]	[illegible]	[illegible]	[illegible]	[illegible]	[illegible]	[illegible]	Meath.
[illegible]	[illegible]	[illegible]	[illegible]	[illegible]	[illegible]	[illegible]	[illegible]	[illegible]	[illegible]	[illegible]	[illegible]	[illegible]	[illegible]	Queen's.
[illegible]	[illegible]	[illegible]	[illegible]	[illegible]	[illegible]	[illegible]	[illegible]	[illegible]	[illegible]	[illegible]	[illegible]	[illegible]	[illegible]	Westmeath.
[illegible]	[illegible]	[illegible]	[illegible]	[illegible]	[illegible]	[illegible]	[illegible]	[illegible]	[illegible]	[illegible]	[illegible]	[illegible]	[illegible]	Wexford.
[illegible]	[illegible]	[illegible]	[illegible]	[illegible]	[illegible]	[illegible]	[illegible]	[illegible]	[illegible]	[illegible]	[illegible]	[illegible]	[illegible]	Wicklow.
[illegible]	[illegible]	[illegible]	[illegible]	[illegible]	[illegible]	[illegible]	[illegible]	[illegible]	[illegible]	[illegible]	[illegible]	[illegible]	[illegible]	TOTAL OF LEINSTER.
														MUNSTER:
[illegible]	[illegible]	[illegible]	[illegible]	[illegible]	[illegible]	[illegible]	[illegible]	[illegible]	[illegible]	[illegible]	[illegible]	[illegible]	[illegible]	Clare.
[illegible]	[illegible]	[illegible]	[illegible]	[illegible]	[illegible]	[illegible]	[illegible]	[illegible]	[illegible]	[illegible]	[illegible]	[illegible]	[illegible]	Cork.
[illegible]	[illegible]	[illegible]	[illegible]	[illegible]	[illegible]	[illegible]	[illegible]	[illegible]	[illegible]	[illegible]	[illegible]	[illegible]	[illegible]	Kerry.
[illegible]	[illegible]	[illegible]	[illegible]	[illegible]	[illegible]	[illegible]	[illegible]	[illegible]	[illegible]	[illegible]	[illegible]	[illegible]	[illegible]	Limerick.
[illegible]	[illegible]	[illegible]	[illegible]	[illegible]	[illegible]	[illegible]	[illegible]	[illegible]	[illegible]	[illegible]	[illegible]	[illegible]	[illegible]	Tipperary.
[illegible]	[illegible]	[illegible]	[illegible]	[illegible]	[illegible]	[illegible]	[illegible]	[illegible]	[illegible]	[illegible]	[illegible]	[illegible]	[illegible]	Waterford.
[illegible]	[illegible]	[illegible]	[illegible]	[illegible]	[illegible]	[illegible]	[illegible]	[illegible]	[illegible]	[illegible]	[illegible]	[illegible]	[illegible]	TOTAL OF MUNSTER.
														ULSTER:
[illegible]	[illegible]	[illegible]	[illegible]	[illegible]	[illegible]	[illegible]	[illegible]	[illegible]	[illegible]	[illegible]	[illegible]	[illegible]	[illegible]	Antrim.
[illegible]	[illegible]	[illegible]	[illegible]	[illegible]	[illegible]	[illegible]	[illegible]	[illegible]	[illegible]	[illegible]	[illegible]	[illegible]	[illegible]	Armagh.
[illegible]	[illegible]	[illegible]	[illegible]	[illegible]	[illegible]	[illegible]	[illegible]	[illegible]	[illegible]	[illegible]	[illegible]	[illegible]	[illegible]	Cavan.
[illegible]	[illegible]	[illegible]	[illegible]	[illegible]	[illegible]	[illegible]	[illegible]	[illegible]	[illegible]	[illegible]	[illegible]	[illegible]	[illegible]	Donegal.
[illegible]	[illegible]	[illegible]	[illegible]	[illegible]	[illegible]	[illegible]	[illegible]	[illegible]	[illegible]	[illegible]	[illegible]	[illegible]	[illegible]	Down.
[illegible]	[illegible]	[illegible]	[illegible]	[illegible]	[illegible]	[illegible]	[illegible]	[illegible]	[illegible]	[illegible]	[illegible]	[illegible]	[illegible]	Fermanagh.
[illegible]	[illegible]	[illegible]	[illegible]	[illegible]	[illegible]	[illegible]	[illegible]	[illegible]	[illegible]	[illegible]	[illegible]	[illegible]	[illegible]	Londonderry.
[illegible]	[illegible]	[illegible]	[illegible]	[illegible]	[illegible]	[illegible]	[illegible]	[illegible]	[illegible]	[illegible]	[illegible]	[illegible]	[illegible]	Monaghan.
[illegible]	[illegible]	[illegible]	[illegible]	[illegible]	[illegible]	[illegible]	[illegible]	[illegible]	[illegible]	[illegible]	[illegible]	[illegible]	[illegible]	Tyrone.
[illegible]	[illegible]	[illegible]	[illegible]	[illegible]	[illegible]	[illegible]	[illegible]	[illegible]	[illegible]	[illegible]	[illegible]	[illegible]	[illegible]	TOTAL OF ULSTER.
														CONNAUGHT:
[illegible]	[illegible]	[illegible]	[illegible]	[illegible]	[illegible]	[illegible]	[illegible]	[illegible]	[illegible]	[illegible]	[illegible]	[illegible]	[illegible]	Galway.
[illegible]	[illegible]	[illegible]	[illegible]	[illegible]	[illegible]	[illegible]	[illegible]	[illegible]	[illegible]	[illegible]	[illegible]	[illegible]	[illegible]	Leitrim.
[illegible]	[illegible]	[illegible]	[illegible]	[illegible]	[illegible]	[illegible]	[illegible]	[illegible]	[illegible]	[illegible]	[illegible]	[illegible]	[illegible]	Mayo.
[illegible]	[illegible]	[illegible]	[illegible]	[illegible]	[illegible]	[illegible]	[illegible]	[illegible]	[illegible]	[illegible]	[illegible]	[illegible]	[illegible]	Roscommon.
[illegible]	[illegible]	[illegible]	[illegible]	[illegible]	[illegible]	[illegible]	[illegible]	[illegible]	[illegible]	[illegible]	[illegible]	[illegible]	[illegible]	Sligo.
[illegible]	[illegible]	[illegible]	[illegible]	[illegible]	[illegible]	[illegible]	[illegible]	[illegible]	[illegible]	[illegible]	[illegible]	[illegible]	[illegible]	TOTAL OF CONNAUGHT.
[illegible]	[illegible]	[illegible]	[illegible]	[illegible]	[illegible]	[illegible]	[illegible]	[illegible]	[illegible]	[illegible]	[illegible]	[illegible]	[illegible]	TOTAL OF IRELAND.

PRODUCE PER STATUTE ACRE, AND THE TOTAL PRODUCE OF IRELAND TO 1873, INCLUSIVE.

Potatoes			Turnips			Mangel Wurzel			Cabbage			Flax			Hay				
[illegible]	[illegible]	[illegible]	[illegible]	[illegible]	[illegible]	[illegible]	[illegible]	[illegible]	[illegible]	[illegible]	[illegible]	[illegible]	[illegible]	[illegible]	[illegible]	[illegible]	[illegible]	[illegible]	[illegible]

[illegible]

LEINSTER AND MUNSTER.

ESTIMATED AVERAGE PRODUCE PER STATUTE ACRE, AND TOTAL PRODUCE, OF THE ... OFFICERS OF THE ROYAL IRISH CONSTABULARY AND METROPOLITAN POLICE:

Provinces and Counties.	Wheat: Average per acre	Wheat: Total produce	Oats: Average per acre	Oats: Total produce	Barley: Average per acre	Barley: Total produce	Bere: Average per acre	Bere: Total produce	Rye: Average per acre	Rye: Total produce	Beans: Average per acre	Beans: Total produce
LEINSTER:												
Carlow, 1872 / 1873	[illegible]	[illegible]	[illegible]	[illegible]	[illegible]	[illegible]	[illegible]	[illegible]	[illegible]	[illegible]	[illegible]	[illegible]
Dublin, 1872 / 1873	[illegible]	[illegible]	[illegible]	[illegible]	[illegible]	[illegible]	[illegible]	[illegible]	[illegible]	[illegible]	[illegible]	[illegible]
Kildare, 1872 / 1873	[illegible]	[illegible]	[illegible]	[illegible]	[illegible]	[illegible]	[illegible]	[illegible]	[illegible]	[illegible]	[illegible]	[illegible]
Kilkenny, 1872 / 1873	[illegible]	[illegible]	[illegible]	[illegible]	[illegible]	[illegible]	[illegible]	[illegible]	[illegible]	[illegible]	[illegible]	[illegible]
King's, 1872 / 1873	[illegible]	[illegible]	[illegible]	[illegible]	[illegible]	[illegible]	[illegible]	[illegible]	[illegible]	[illegible]	[illegible]	[illegible]
Longford, 1872 / 1873	[illegible]	[illegible]	[illegible]	[illegible]	[illegible]	[illegible]	[illegible]	[illegible]	[illegible]	[illegible]	[illegible]	[illegible]
Louth, 1872 / 1873	[illegible]	[illegible]	[illegible]	[illegible]	[illegible]	[illegible]	[illegible]	[illegible]	[illegible]	[illegible]	[illegible]	[illegible]
Meath, 1872 / 1873	[illegible]	[illegible]	[illegible]	[illegible]	[illegible]	[illegible]	[illegible]	[illegible]	[illegible]	[illegible]	[illegible]	[illegible]
Queen's, 1872 / 1873	[illegible]	[illegible]	[illegible]	[illegible]	[illegible]	[illegible]	[illegible]	[illegible]	[illegible]	[illegible]	[illegible]	[illegible]
Westmeath, 1872 / 1873	[illegible]	[illegible]	[illegible]	[illegible]	[illegible]	[illegible]	[illegible]	[illegible]	[illegible]	[illegible]	[illegible]	[illegible]
Wexford, 1872 / 1873	[illegible]	[illegible]	[illegible]	[illegible]	[illegible]	[illegible]	[illegible]	[illegible]	[illegible]	[illegible]	[illegible]	[illegible]
Wicklow, 1872 / 1873	[illegible]	[illegible]	[illegible]	[illegible]	[illegible]	[illegible]	[illegible]	[illegible]	[illegible]	[illegible]	[illegible]	[illegible]
Total of Leinster, 1872 / 1873	[illegible]	[illegible]	[illegible]	[illegible]	[illegible]	[illegible]	[illegible]	[illegible]	[illegible]	[illegible]	[illegible]	[illegible]
MUNSTER:												
Clare, 1872 / 1873	[illegible]	[illegible]	[illegible]	[illegible]	[illegible]	[illegible]	[illegible]	[illegible]	[illegible]	[illegible]	[illegible]	[illegible]
Cork, 1872 / 1873	[illegible]	[illegible]	[illegible]	[illegible]	[illegible]	[illegible]	[illegible]	[illegible]	[illegible]	[illegible]	[illegible]	[illegible]
Kerry, 1872 / 1873	[illegible]	[illegible]	[illegible]	[illegible]	[illegible]	[illegible]	[illegible]	[illegible]	[illegible]	[illegible]	[illegible]	[illegible]
Limerick, 1872 / 1873	[illegible]	[illegible]	[illegible]	[illegible]	[illegible]	[illegible]	[illegible]	[illegible]	[illegible]	[illegible]	[illegible]	[illegible]
Tipperary, 1872 / 1873	[illegible]	[illegible]	[illegible]	[illegible]	[illegible]	[illegible]	[illegible]	[illegible]	[illegible]	[illegible]	[illegible]	[illegible]
Waterford, 1872 / 1873	[illegible]	[illegible]	[illegible]	[illegible]	[illegible]	[illegible]	[illegible]	[illegible]	[illegible]	[illegible]	[illegible]	[illegible]
Total of Munster, 1872 / 1873	[illegible]	[illegible]	[illegible]	[illegible]	[illegible]	[illegible]	[illegible]	[illegible]	[illegible]	[illegible]	[illegible]	[illegible]

ACREAGE UNDER EACH OF THE

Provinces and Counties.	Wheat.	Oats.	Barley.	Bere.	Rye.	Beans.	Peas.	Potatoes.	Turnips.	Mangel Wurzel.	Cabbage.	Flax.	Hay.	Total.
LEINSTER:														
Carlow, 1872 / 1873	[illegible]	[illegible]	[illegible]	[illegible]	[illegible]	[illegible]	[illegible]	[illegible]	[illegible]	[illegible]	[illegible]	[illegible]	[illegible]	[illegible]
Dublin, 1872 / 1873	[illegible]	[illegible]	[illegible]	[illegible]	[illegible]	[illegible]	[illegible]	[illegible]	[illegible]	[illegible]	[illegible]	[illegible]	[illegible]	[illegible]
Kildare, 1872 / 1873	[illegible]	[illegible]	[illegible]	[illegible]	[illegible]	[illegible]	[illegible]	[illegible]	[illegible]	[illegible]	[illegible]	[illegible]	[illegible]	[illegible]
Kilkenny, 1872 / 1873	[illegible]	[illegible]	[illegible]	[illegible]	[illegible]	[illegible]	[illegible]	[illegible]	[illegible]	[illegible]	[illegible]	[illegible]	[illegible]	[illegible]
King's, 1872 / 1873	[illegible]	[illegible]	[illegible]	[illegible]	[illegible]	[illegible]	[illegible]	[illegible]	[illegible]	[illegible]	[illegible]	[illegible]	[illegible]	[illegible]
Longford, 1872 / 1873	[illegible]	[illegible]	[illegible]	[illegible]	[illegible]	[illegible]	[illegible]	[illegible]	[illegible]	[illegible]	[illegible]	[illegible]	[illegible]	[illegible]
Louth, 1872 / 1873	[illegible]	[illegible]	[illegible]	[illegible]	[illegible]	[illegible]	[illegible]	[illegible]	[illegible]	[illegible]	[illegible]	[illegible]	[illegible]	[illegible]
Meath, 1872 / 1873	[illegible]	[illegible]	[illegible]	[illegible]	[illegible]	[illegible]	[illegible]	[illegible]	[illegible]	[illegible]	[illegible]	[illegible]	[illegible]	[illegible]
Queen's, 1872 / 1873	[illegible]	[illegible]	[illegible]	[illegible]	[illegible]	[illegible]	[illegible]	[illegible]	[illegible]	[illegible]	[illegible]	[illegible]	[illegible]	[illegible]
Westmeath, 1872 / 1873	[illegible]	[illegible]	[illegible]	[illegible]	[illegible]	[illegible]	[illegible]	[illegible]	[illegible]	[illegible]	[illegible]	[illegible]	[illegible]	[illegible]

LEINSTER AND MUNSTER.

… CROPS IN 1872 AND 1873; COMPILED FROM RETURNS RECEIVED FROM THE … ACREAGE UNDER EACH OF THESE CROPS IN THE SAME YEARS.

Green Crops													
Potatoes		Turnips		Mangel Wurzel		Cabbage		Flax		Hay		Provinces and Counties	
Average produce per acre	Estimated total produce	Average produce per acre	Estimated total produce	Average produce per acre	Estimated total produce	Average produce per acre	Estimated total produce	Average produce per acre	Estimated total produce	Average produce per acre	Estimated total produce		
Tons	Tons	Tons	Tons	Tons	Tons	Tons	Tons	Stones	Stones	Tons	Tons	Leinster:	
[illegible]	[illegible]	[illegible]	[illegible]	[illegible]	[illegible]	[illegible]	[illegible]	[illegible]	[illegible]	[illegible]	[illegible]	1872	Carlow
[illegible]	[illegible]	[illegible]	[illegible]	[illegible]	[illegible]	[illegible]	[illegible]	[illegible]	[illegible]	[illegible]	[illegible]	1873	
[illegible]	[illegible]	[illegible]	[illegible]	[illegible]	[illegible]	[illegible]	[illegible]	[illegible]	[illegible]	[illegible]	[illegible]	1872	Dublin
[illegible]	[illegible]	[illegible]	[illegible]	[illegible]	[illegible]	[illegible]	[illegible]			[illegible]	[illegible]	1873	
[illegible]	[illegible]	[illegible]	[illegible]	[illegible]	[illegible]	[illegible]	[illegible]	[illegible]	[illegible]	[illegible]	[illegible]	1872	Kildare
[illegible]	[illegible]	[illegible]	[illegible]	[illegible]	[illegible]	[illegible]	[illegible]	[illegible]	[illegible]	[illegible]	[illegible]	1873	
[illegible]	[illegible]	[illegible]	[illegible]	[illegible]	[illegible]	[illegible]	[illegible]	[illegible]	[illegible]	[illegible]	[illegible]	1872	Kilkenny
[illegible]	[illegible]	[illegible]	[illegible]	[illegible]	[illegible]	[illegible]	[illegible]	[illegible]	[illegible]	[illegible]	[illegible]	1873	
[illegible]	[illegible]	[illegible]	[illegible]	[illegible]	[illegible]	[illegible]	[illegible]	[illegible]	[illegible]	[illegible]	[illegible]	1872	King's
[illegible]	[illegible]	[illegible]	[illegible]	[illegible]	[illegible]	[illegible]	[illegible]	[illegible]	[illegible]	[illegible]	[illegible]	1873	
[illegible]	[illegible]	[illegible]	[illegible]	[illegible]	[illegible]	[illegible]	[illegible]	[illegible]	[illegible]	[illegible]	[illegible]	1872	Longford
[illegible]	[illegible]	[illegible]	[illegible]	[illegible]	[illegible]	[illegible]	[illegible]	[illegible]	[illegible]	[illegible]	[illegible]	1873	
[illegible]	[illegible]	[illegible]	[illegible]	[illegible]	[illegible]	[illegible]	[illegible]	[illegible]	[illegible]	[illegible]	[illegible]	1872	Louth
[illegible]	[illegible]	[illegible]	[illegible]	[illegible]	[illegible]	[illegible]	[illegible]	[illegible]	[illegible]	[illegible]	[illegible]	1873	
[illegible]	[illegible]	[illegible]	[illegible]	[illegible]	[illegible]	[illegible]	[illegible]	[illegible]	[illegible]	[illegible]	[illegible]	1872	Meath
[illegible]	[illegible]	[illegible]	[illegible]	[illegible]	[illegible]	[illegible]	[illegible]	[illegible]	[illegible]	[illegible]	[illegible]	1873	
[illegible]	[illegible]	[illegible]	[illegible]	[illegible]	[illegible]	[illegible]	[illegible]	[illegible]	[illegible]	[illegible]	[illegible]	1872	Queen's
[illegible]	[illegible]	[illegible]	[illegible]	[illegible]	[illegible]	[illegible]	[illegible]	[illegible]	[illegible]	[illegible]	[illegible]	1873	
[illegible]	[illegible]	[illegible]	[illegible]	[illegible]	[illegible]	[illegible]	[illegible]	[illegible]	[illegible]	[illegible]	[illegible]	1872	Westmeath
[illegible]	[illegible]	[illegible]	[illegible]	[illegible]	[illegible]	[illegible]	[illegible]	[illegible]	[illegible]	[illegible]	[illegible]	1873	
[illegible]	[illegible]	[illegible]	[illegible]	[illegible]	[illegible]	[illegible]	[illegible]	[illegible]	[illegible]	[illegible]	[illegible]	1872	Wexford
[illegible]	[illegible]	[illegible]	[illegible]	[illegible]	[illegible]	[illegible]	[illegible]	[illegible]	[illegible]	[illegible]	[illegible]	1873	
[illegible]	[illegible]	[illegible]	[illegible]	[illegible]	[illegible]	[illegible]	[illegible]	-	-	[illegible]	[illegible]	1872	Wicklow
[illegible]	[illegible]	[illegible]	[illegible]	[illegible]	[illegible]	[illegible]	[illegible]	-	-	[illegible]	[illegible]	1873	

Provinces and Counties	Wheat		Oats		Barley		Bere		Rye		Beans	
	[illegible]	[illegible]	[illegible]	[illegible]	[illegible]	[illegible]	[illegible]	[illegible]	[illegible]	[illegible]	[illegible]	[illegible]
ULSTER:												
Antrim	[illegible]	[illegible]	[illegible]	[illegible]	[illegible]	[illegible]	[illegible]	[illegible]	[illegible]	[illegible]	[illegible]	[illegible]
Armagh	[illegible]	[illegible]	[illegible]	[illegible]	[illegible]	[illegible]	[illegible]	[illegible]	[illegible]	[illegible]	[illegible]	[illegible]
Cavan	[illegible]	[illegible]	[illegible]	[illegible]	[illegible]	[illegible]	[illegible]	[illegible]	[illegible]	[illegible]	[illegible]	[illegible]
Donegal	[illegible]	[illegible]	[illegible]	[illegible]	[illegible]	[illegible]	[illegible]	[illegible]	[illegible]	[illegible]	[illegible]	[illegible]
Down	[illegible]	[illegible]	[illegible]	[illegible]	[illegible]	[illegible]	[illegible]	[illegible]	[illegible]	[illegible]	[illegible]	[illegible]
Fermanagh	[illegible]	[illegible]	[illegible]	[illegible]	[illegible]	[illegible]	[illegible]	[illegible]	[illegible]	[illegible]	[illegible]	[illegible]
Londonderry	[illegible]	[illegible]	[illegible]	[illegible]	[illegible]	[illegible]	[illegible]	[illegible]	[illegible]	[illegible]	[illegible]	[illegible]
Monaghan	[illegible]	[illegible]	[illegible]	[illegible]	[illegible]	[illegible]	[illegible]	[illegible]	[illegible]	[illegible]	[illegible]	[illegible]
Tyrone	[illegible]	[illegible]	[illegible]	[illegible]	[illegible]	[illegible]	[illegible]	[illegible]	[illegible]	[illegible]	[illegible]	[illegible]
Total of Ulster	[illegible]	[illegible]	[illegible]	[illegible]	[illegible]	[illegible]	[illegible]	[illegible]	[illegible]	[illegible]	[illegible]	[illegible]
CONNAUGHT:												
Galway	[illegible]	[illegible]	[illegible]	[illegible]	[illegible]	[illegible]	[illegible]	[illegible]	[illegible]	[illegible]	[illegible]	[illegible]
Leitrim	[illegible]	[illegible]	[illegible]	[illegible]	[illegible]	[illegible]	[illegible]	[illegible]	[illegible]	[illegible]	[illegible]	[illegible]
Mayo	[illegible]	[illegible]	[illegible]	[illegible]	[illegible]	[illegible]	[illegible]	[illegible]	[illegible]	[illegible]	[illegible]	[illegible]
Roscommon	[illegible]	[illegible]	[illegible]	[illegible]	[illegible]	[illegible]	[illegible]	[illegible]	[illegible]	[illegible]	[illegible]	[illegible]
Sligo	[illegible]	[illegible]	[illegible]	[illegible]	[illegible]	[illegible]	[illegible]	[illegible]	[illegible]	[illegible]	[illegible]	[illegible]
Total of Connaught	[illegible]	[illegible]	[illegible]	[illegible]	[illegible]	[illegible]	[illegible]	[illegible]	[illegible]	[illegible]	[illegible]	[illegible]
Total of Ireland	[illegible]	[illegible]	[illegible]	[illegible]	[illegible]	[illegible]	[illegible]	[illegible]	[illegible]	[illegible]	[illegible]	[illegible]

ACREAGE UNDER EACH OF THE

Provinces and Counties	Wheat	Oats	Barley	Bere	Rye	Beans	Peas	Potatoes	Turnips	Mangel Wurzel	Cabbage	Flax	Hay	Total
ULSTER:														
Antrim	[illegible]	[illegible]	[illegible]	[illegible]	[illegible]	[illegible]	[illegible]	[illegible]	[illegible]	[illegible]	[illegible]	[illegible]	[illegible]	[illegible]
Armagh	[illegible]	[illegible]	[illegible]	[illegible]	[illegible]	[illegible]	[illegible]	[illegible]	[illegible]	[illegible]	[illegible]	[illegible]	[illegible]	[illegible]
Cavan	[illegible]	[illegible]	[illegible]	[illegible]	[illegible]	[illegible]	[illegible]	[illegible]	[illegible]	[illegible]	[illegible]	[illegible]	[illegible]	[illegible]
Donegal	[illegible]	[illegible]	[illegible]	[illegible]	[illegible]	[illegible]	[illegible]	[illegible]	[illegible]	[illegible]	[illegible]	[illegible]	[illegible]	[illegible]
Down	[illegible]	[illegible]	[illegible]	[illegible]	[illegible]	[illegible]	[illegible]	[illegible]	[illegible]	[illegible]	[illegible]	[illegible]	[illegible]	[illegible]
Fermanagh	[illegible]	[illegible]	[illegible]	[illegible]	[illegible]	[illegible]	[illegible]	[illegible]	[illegible]	[illegible]	[illegible]	[illegible]	[illegible]	[illegible]
Londonderry	[illegible]	[illegible]	[illegible]	[illegible]	[illegible]	[illegible]	[illegible]	[illegible]	[illegible]	[illegible]	[illegible]	[illegible]	[illegible]	[illegible]
Monaghan	[illegible]	[illegible]	[illegible]	[illegible]	[illegible]	[illegible]	[illegible]	[illegible]	[illegible]	[illegible]	[illegible]	[illegible]	[illegible]	[illegible]

ULSTER AND CONNAUGHT.

FOLLOWING CROPS IN 1878 AND 1879; COMPILED FROM RETURNS RECEIVED FROM THE ALSO THE ACREAGE UNDER EACH OF THESE CROPS IN THE SAME YEARS—*continued.*

Peas: Average Produce per Statute Acre	Peas: Estimated Total Produce	Potatoes: Average Produce per Statute Acre	Potatoes: Estimated Total Produce	Turnips: Average Produce per Statute Acre	Turnips: Estimated Total Produce	Mangel Wurzel: Average Produce per Statute Acre	Mangel Wurzel: Estimated Total Produce	Cabbage: Average Produce per Statute Acre	Cabbage: Estimated Total Produce	Flax: Average Produce per Statute Acre	Flax: Estimated Total Produce	Hay: Average Produce per Statute Acre	Hay: Estimated Total Produce	Year	Provinces and Counties
bus.	Qrs.	Tons.	Tons.	Tons.	Tons.	Tons.	Tons.	Tons.	Tons.	Stones of 14 lbs.	Stones of 14 lbs.	Tons.	Tons.		ULSTER.
[illegible]	[illegible]	[illegible]	[illegible]	[illegible]	[illegible]	[illegible]	[illegible]	[illegible]	[illegible]	[illegible]	[illegible]	[illegible]	[illegible]	1878, 1879,	Antrim.
[illegible]	[illegible]	[illegible]	[illegible]	[illegible]	[illegible]	[illegible]	[illegible]	[illegible]	[illegible]	[illegible]	[illegible]	[illegible]	[illegible]	1878, 1879,	Armagh.
[illegible]	[illegible]	[illegible]	[illegible]	[illegible]	[illegible]	[illegible]	[illegible]	[illegible]	[illegible]	[illegible]	[illegible]	[illegible]	[illegible]	1878, 1879,	Cavan.
[illegible]	[illegible]	[illegible]	[illegible]	[illegible]	[illegible]	[illegible]	[illegible]	[illegible]	[illegible]	[illegible]	[illegible]	[illegible]	[illegible]	1878, 1879,	Donegal.
[illegible]	[illegible]	[illegible]	[illegible]	[illegible]	[illegible]	[illegible]	[illegible]	[illegible]	[illegible]	[illegible]	[illegible]	[illegible]	[illegible]	1878, 1879,	Down.
[illegible]	[illegible]	[illegible]	[illegible]	[illegible]	[illegible]	[illegible]	[illegible]	[illegible]	[illegible]	[illegible]	[illegible]	[illegible]	[illegible]	1878, 1879,	Fermanagh.
[illegible]	[illegible]	[illegible]	[illegible]	[illegible]	[illegible]	[illegible]	[illegible]	[illegible]	[illegible]	[illegible]	[illegible]	[illegible]	[illegible]	1878, 1879,	Londonderry.
[illegible]	[illegible]	[illegible]	[illegible]	[illegible]	[illegible]	[illegible]	[illegible]	[illegible]	[illegible]	[illegible]	[illegible]	[illegible]	[illegible]	1878, 1879,	Monaghan.
[illegible]	[illegible]	[illegible]	[illegible]	[illegible]	[illegible]	[illegible]	[illegible]	[illegible]	[illegible]	[illegible]	[illegible]	[illegible]	[illegible]	1878, 1879,	Tyrone.
[illegible]	[illegible]	[illegible]	[illegible]	[illegible]	[illegible]	[illegible]	[illegible]	[illegible]	[illegible]	[illegible]	[illegible]	[illegible]	[illegible]	1878, 1879,	Total of Ulster.
															CONNAUGHT.
[illegible]	[illegible]	[illegible]	[illegible]	[illegible]	[illegible]	[illegible]	[illegible]	[illegible]	[illegible]	[illegible]	[illegible]	[illegible]	[illegible]	1878, 1879,	Galway.
[illegible]	[illegible]	[illegible]	[illegible]	[illegible]	[illegible]	[illegible]	[illegible]	[illegible]	[illegible]	[illegible]	[illegible]	[illegible]	[illegible]	1878, 1879,	Leitrim.
[illegible]	[illegible]	[illegible]	[illegible]	[illegible]	[illegible]	[illegible]	[illegible]	[illegible]	[illegible]	[illegible]	[illegible]	[illegible]	[illegible]	1878, 1879,	Mayo.
[illegible]	[illegible]	[illegible]	[illegible]	[illegible]	[illegible]	[illegible]	[illegible]	[illegible]	[illegible]	[illegible]	[illegible]	[illegible]	[illegible]	1878, 1879,	Roscommon.
[illegible]	[illegible]	[illegible]	[illegible]	[illegible]	[illegible]	[illegible]	[illegible]	[illegible]	[illegible]	[illegible]	[illegible]	[illegible]	[illegible]	1878, 1879,	Sligo.
[illegible]	[illegible]	[illegible]	[illegible]	[illegible]	[illegible]	[illegible]	[illegible]	[illegible]	[illegible]	[illegible]	[illegible]	[illegible]	[illegible]	1878, 1879,	Total of Connaught.
[illegible]	[illegible]	[illegible]	[illegible]	[illegible]	[illegible]	[illegible]	[illegible]	[illegible]	[illegible]	[illegible]	[illegible]	[illegible]	[illegible]	1878, 1879,	Total of Ireland.

FOREGOING CROPS, IN STATUTE MEASURE.

Provinces and Counties	Year	Wheat	Oats	Barley	Bere	Rye	Beans	Peas	Potatoes	Turnips	Mangel Wurzel	Cabbage	Flax	Hay	Total
		Acres	Acres	Acres	Acres	Acres	Acres	Acres	Acres	Acres	Acres	Acres	Acres	Acres	Acres
ULSTER—continued.															
Tyrone	1878, 1879,	[illegible]	[illegible]	[illegible]	[illegible]	[illegible]	[illegible]	[illegible]	[illegible]	[illegible]	[illegible]	[illegible]	[illegible]	[illegible]	[illegible]
Total of Ulster,	1878, 1879,	[illegible]	[illegible]	[illegible]	[illegible]	[illegible]	[illegible]	[illegible]	[illegible]	[illegible]	[illegible]	[illegible]	[illegible]	[illegible]	[illegible]
CONNAUGHT.															
Galway	1878, 1879,	[illegible]	[illegible]	[illegible]	[illegible]	[illegible]	[illegible]	[illegible]	[illegible]	[illegible]	[illegible]	[illegible]	[illegible]	[illegible]	[illegible]
Leitrim	1878, 1879,	[illegible]	[illegible]	[illegible]	[illegible]	[illegible]	[illegible]	[illegible]	[illegible]	[illegible]	[illegible]	[illegible]	[illegible]	[illegible]	[illegible]
Mayo	1878, 1879,	[illegible]	[illegible]	[illegible]	[illegible]	[illegible]	[illegible]	[illegible]	[illegible]	[illegible]	[illegible]	[illegible]	[illegible]	[illegible]	[illegible]
Roscommon	1878, 1879,	[illegible]	[illegible]	[illegible]	[illegible]	[illegible]	[illegible]	[illegible]	[illegible]	[illegible]	[illegible]	[illegible]	[illegible]	[illegible]	[illegible]
Sligo	1878, 1879,	[illegible]	[illegible]	[illegible]	[illegible]	[illegible]	[illegible]	[illegible]	[illegible]	[illegible]	[illegible]	[illegible]	[illegible]	[illegible]	[illegible]
Total of Connaught,	1878, 1879,	[illegible]	[illegible]	[illegible]	[illegible]	[illegible]	[illegible]	[illegible]	[illegible]	[illegible]	[illegible]	[illegible]	[illegible]	[illegible]	[illegible]

GENERAL ABSTRACT showing the ACREAGE under the several CROPS, in STATUTE MEASURE; the TOTAL PRODUCE of each CROP; and the INCREASE or DECREASE in the PRODUCE, between 1872 and 1873; by PROVINCES, and for all IRELAND.

Provinces.	Description of Crops.	Cereal Crops: Acreage under Crops, 1872	1873	Estimated Quantity of Produce, 1872	1873	Difference of Produce between 1872 and 1873: Increase	Decrease	Description of Crops.	Green Crops: Acreage under Crops, 1872	1873	Estimated Quantity of Produce, 1872	1873	Difference of Produce between 1872 and 1873: Increase	Decrease
LEINSTER.	Wheat,	[illegible]	[illegible]	[illegible]	[illegible]	[illegible]	[illegible]	Potatoes,	[illegible]	[illegible]	[illegible]	[illegible]	[illegible]	[illegible]
	Oats,	[illegible]	[illegible]	[illegible]	[illegible]	[illegible]	[illegible]	Turnips,	[illegible]	[illegible]	[illegible]	[illegible]	[illegible]	[illegible]
	Barley,	[illegible]	[illegible]	[illegible]	[illegible]	[illegible]	[illegible]	Mangel,	[illegible]	[illegible]	[illegible]	[illegible]	[illegible]	[illegible]
	Bere,	[illegible]	[illegible]	[illegible]	[illegible]	[illegible]	[illegible]	Cabbage,	[illegible]	[illegible]	[illegible]	[illegible]	[illegible]	[illegible]
	Rye,	[illegible]	[illegible]	[illegible]	[illegible]	[illegible]	[illegible]	Flax,	[illegible]	[illegible]	[illegible]	[illegible]	[illegible]	[illegible]
	Beans,	[illegible]	[illegible]	[illegible]	[illegible]	[illegible]	[illegible]	Meadow,	[illegible]	[illegible]	[illegible]	[illegible]	[illegible]	[illegible]
	Peas,	[illegible]	[illegible]	[illegible]	[illegible]	[illegible]	[illegible]							
MUNSTER.	Wheat,	[illegible]	[illegible]	[illegible]	[illegible]	[illegible]	[illegible]	Potatoes,	[illegible]	[illegible]	[illegible]	[illegible]	[illegible]	[illegible]
	Oats,	[illegible]	[illegible]	[illegible]	[illegible]	[illegible]	[illegible]	Turnips,	[illegible]	[illegible]	[illegible]	[illegible]	[illegible]	[illegible]
	Barley,	[illegible]	[illegible]	[illegible]	[illegible]	[illegible]	[illegible]	Mangel,	[illegible]	[illegible]	[illegible]	[illegible]	[illegible]	[illegible]
	Bere,	[illegible]	[illegible]	[illegible]	[illegible]	[illegible]	[illegible]	Cabbage,	[illegible]	[illegible]	[illegible]	[illegible]	[illegible]	[illegible]
	Rye,	[illegible]	[illegible]	[illegible]	[illegible]	[illegible]	[illegible]	Flax,	[illegible]	[illegible]	[illegible]	[illegible]	[illegible]	[illegible]
	Beans,	[illegible]	[illegible]	[illegible]	[illegible]	[illegible]	[illegible]	Meadow,	[illegible]	[illegible]	[illegible]	[illegible]	[illegible]	[illegible]
	Peas,	[illegible]	[illegible]	[illegible]	[illegible]	[illegible]	[illegible]							
ULSTER.	Wheat,	[illegible]	[illegible]	[illegible]	[illegible]	[illegible]	[illegible]	Potatoes,	[illegible]	[illegible]	[illegible]	[illegible]	[illegible]	[illegible]
	Oats,	[illegible]	[illegible]	[illegible]	[illegible]	[illegible]	[illegible]	Turnips,	[illegible]	[illegible]	[illegible]	[illegible]	[illegible]	[illegible]
	Barley,	[illegible]	[illegible]	[illegible]	[illegible]	[illegible]	[illegible]	Mangel,	[illegible]	[illegible]	[illegible]	[illegible]	[illegible]	[illegible]
	Bere,	[illegible]	[illegible]	[illegible]	[illegible]	[illegible]	[illegible]	Cabbage,	[illegible]	[illegible]	[illegible]	[illegible]	[illegible]	[illegible]
	Rye,	[illegible]	[illegible]	[illegible]	[illegible]	[illegible]	[illegible]	Flax,	[illegible]	[illegible]	[illegible]	[illegible]	[illegible]	[illegible]
	Beans,	[illegible]	[illegible]	[illegible]	[illegible]	[illegible]	[illegible]	Meadow,	[illegible]	[illegible]	[illegible]	[illegible]	[illegible]	[illegible]
	Peas,	[illegible]	[illegible]	[illegible]	[illegible]	[illegible]	[illegible]							
CONNAUGHT.	Wheat,	[illegible]	[illegible]	[illegible]	[illegible]	[illegible]	[illegible]	Potatoes,	[illegible]	[illegible]	[illegible]	[illegible]	[illegible]	[illegible]
	Oats,	[illegible]	[illegible]	[illegible]	[illegible]	[illegible]	[illegible]	Turnips,	[illegible]	[illegible]	[illegible]	[illegible]	[illegible]	[illegible]
	Barley,	[illegible]	[illegible]	[illegible]	[illegible]	[illegible]	[illegible]	Mangel,	[illegible]	[illegible]	[illegible]	[illegible]	[illegible]	[illegible]
	Bere,	[illegible]	[illegible]	[illegible]	[illegible]	[illegible]	[illegible]	Cabbage,	[illegible]	[illegible]	[illegible]	[illegible]	[illegible]	[illegible]
	Rye,	[illegible]	[illegible]	[illegible]	[illegible]	[illegible]	[illegible]	Flax,	[illegible]	[illegible]	[illegible]	[illegible]	[illegible]	[illegible]
	Beans,	[illegible]	[illegible]	[illegible]	[illegible]	[illegible]	[illegible]	Meadow,	[illegible]	[illegible]	[illegible]	[illegible]	[illegible]	[illegible]
	Peas,	[illegible]	[illegible]	[illegible]	[illegible]	[illegible]	[illegible]							
IRELAND.	Wheat,	[illegible]	[illegible]	[illegible]	[illegible]	[illegible]	[illegible]	Potatoes,	[illegible]	[illegible]	[illegible]	[illegible]	[illegible]	[illegible]
	Oats,	[illegible]	[illegible]	[illegible]	[illegible]	[illegible]	[illegible]	Turnips,	[illegible]	[illegible]	[illegible]	[illegible]	[illegible]	[illegible]
	Barley,	[illegible]	[illegible]	[illegible]	[illegible]	[illegible]	[illegible]	Mangel,	[illegible]	[illegible]	[illegible]	[illegible]	[illegible]	[illegible]
	Bere,	[illegible]	[illegible]	[illegible]	[illegible]	[illegible]	[illegible]	Cabbage,	[illegible]	[illegible]	[illegible]	[illegible]	[illegible]	[illegible]
	Rye,	[illegible]	[illegible]	[illegible]	[illegible]	[illegible]	[illegible]	Flax,	[illegible]	[illegible]	[illegible]	[illegible]	[illegible]	[illegible]
	Beans,	[illegible]	[illegible]	[illegible]	[illegible]	[illegible]	[illegible]	Meadow,	[illegible]	[illegible]	[illegible]	[illegible]	[illegible]	[illegible]
	Peas,	[illegible]	[illegible]	[illegible]	[illegible]	[illegible]	[illegible]							

ACREAGE in STATUTE MEASURE, and CEREAL PRODUCE in "QUARTERS," in 1872 and 1873, for all IRELAND.

Description of Crops.	Acreage under Crops, 1872	1873	Estimated Quantity of Produce, 1872	1873	Difference of Produce between 1872 and 1873: Increase	Decrease	Description of Crops.	Acreage under Crops, 1872	1873	Estimated Quantity of Produce, 1872	1873	Difference: Increase	Decrease
Wheat,	[illegible]	[illegible]	[illegible]	[illegible]	[illegible]	[illegible]	Rye,	[illegible]	[illegible]	[illegible]	[illegible]	[illegible]	[illegible]
Oats,	[illegible]	[illegible]	[illegible]	[illegible]	[illegible]	[illegible]	Beans,	[illegible]	[illegible]	[illegible]	[illegible]	[illegible]	[illegible]
Barley,	[illegible]	[illegible]	[illegible]	[illegible]	[illegible]	[illegible]	Peas,	[illegible]	[illegible]	[illegible]	[illegible]	[illegible]	[illegible]
Bere,	[illegible]	[illegible]	[illegible]	[illegible]	[illegible]	[illegible]							

EMIGRATION FROM IRELAND, DURING THE YEAR 1878.

I.—TABLE showing the Number of Male and Female Emigrants, who left the different Ports of Ireland, during each month of the year 1878.

Ports.	January.		February.		March.		April.		May.		June.		July.		August.		September.		October.		November.		December.		Ten-and-Years.		
	M.	F.	M.	F.	M.	F.	M.	F.	M.	F.	M.	F.	M.	F.	M.	F.	M.	F.	M.	F.	M.	F.	M.	F.	Males.	Females.	Total.
[illegible]	[illegible]	[illegible]	[illegible]	[illegible]	[illegible]	[illegible]	[illegible]	[illegible]	[illegible]	[illegible]	[illegible]	[illegible]	[illegible]	[illegible]	[illegible]	[illegible]	[illegible]	[illegible]	[illegible]	[illegible]	[illegible]	[illegible]	[illegible]	[illegible]	[illegible]	[illegible]	[illegible]
General Total.	[illegible]	[illegible]	[illegible]	[illegible]	[illegible]	[illegible]	[illegible]	[illegible]	[illegible]	[illegible]	[illegible]	[illegible]	[illegible]	[illegible]	[illegible]	[illegible]	[illegible]	[illegible]	[illegible]	[illegible]	[illegible]	[illegible]	[illegible]	[illegible]	[illegible]	[illegible]	[illegible]
	[illegible]		[illegible]		[illegible]		[illegible]		[illegible]		[illegible]		[illegible]		[illegible]		[illegible]		[illegible]		[illegible]		[illegible]		[illegible]		

II.—TABLE showing the Number of Male and Female Emigrants from ... those who stated themselves

[illegible]	January M.	January F.	February M.	February F.	March M.	March F.	April M.	April F.	May M.	May F.	June M.	June F.	July M.	July F.
LEINSTER:														
Total from Leinster,	[illegible]	[illegible]	[illegible]	[illegible]	[illegible]	[illegible]	[illegible]	[illegible]	[illegible]	[illegible]	[illegible]	[illegible]	[illegible]	[illegible]
MUNSTER:														
Total from Munster,	[illegible]	[illegible]	[illegible]	[illegible]	[illegible]	[illegible]	[illegible]	[illegible]	[illegible]	[illegible]	[illegible]	[illegible]	[illegible]	[illegible]
ULSTER:														
Total from Ulster,	[illegible]	[illegible]	[illegible]	[illegible]	[illegible]	[illegible]	[illegible]	[illegible]	[illegible]	[illegible]	[illegible]	[illegible]	[illegible]	[illegible]
CONNAUGHT:														
Total from Connaught,	[illegible]	[illegible]	[illegible]	[illegible]	[illegible]	[illegible]	[illegible]	[illegible]	[illegible]	[illegible]	[illegible]	[illegible]	[illegible]	[illegible]
[illegible]	[illegible]	[illegible]	[illegible]	[illegible]	[illegible]	[illegible]	[illegible]	[illegible]	[illegible]	[illegible]	[illegible]	[illegible]	[illegible]	[illegible]
TOTAL FROM IRELAND,	[illegible]	[illegible]	[illegible]	[illegible]	[illegible]	[illegible]	[illegible]	[illegible]	[illegible]	[illegible]	[illegible]	[illegible]	[illegible]	[illegible]
[illegible]														
England and Wales,	[illegible]	[illegible]	[illegible]	[illegible]	[illegible]	[illegible]	[illegible]	[illegible]	[illegible]	[illegible]	[illegible]	[illegible]	[illegible]	[illegible]
Scotland,	[illegible]	[illegible]	[illegible]	[illegible]	[illegible]	[illegible]	[illegible]	[illegible]	[illegible]	[illegible]	[illegible]	[illegible]	[illegible]	[illegible]
The Continent of Europe,	[illegible]	[illegible]	[illegible]	[illegible]	[illegible]	[illegible]	[illegible]	[illegible]	[illegible]	[illegible]	[illegible]	[illegible]	[illegible]	[illegible]
The United States, Canada, and the West Indies,	[illegible]	[illegible]	[illegible]	[illegible]	[illegible]	[illegible]	[illegible]	[illegible]	[illegible]	[illegible]	[illegible]	[illegible]	[illegible]	[illegible]
Asia, Australia, and the East Indies,	[illegible]	[illegible]	[illegible]	[illegible]	[illegible]	[illegible]	[illegible]	[illegible]	[illegible]	[illegible]	[illegible]	[illegible]	[illegible]	[illegible]
GENERAL TOTAL,	[illegible]	[illegible]	[illegible]	[illegible]	[illegible]	[illegible]	[illegible]	[illegible]	[illegible]	[illegible]	[illegible]	[illegible]	[illegible]	[illegible]
	[illegible]		[illegible]		[illegible]		[illegible]		[illegible]		[illegible]		[illegible]	

every County and Province, during each month of the year 1878; also ... to belong to other Countries.

August M.	August F.	September M.	September F.	October M.	October F.	November M.	November F.	December M.	December F.	For the Year Males.	For the Year Females.	For the Year Total.	From what County, Province, or Country.
													Leinster:
[illegible]	[illegible]	[illegible]	[illegible]	[illegible]	[illegible]	[illegible]	[illegible]	[illegible]	[illegible]	[illegible]	[illegible]	[illegible]	[illegible]
[illegible]	[illegible]	[illegible]	[illegible]	[illegible]	[illegible]	[illegible]	[illegible]	[illegible]	[illegible]	[illegible]	[illegible]	[illegible]	Total from Leinster.
													Munster:
[illegible]	[illegible]	[illegible]	[illegible]	[illegible]	[illegible]	[illegible]	[illegible]	[illegible]	[illegible]	[illegible]	[illegible]	[illegible]	[illegible]
[illegible]	[illegible]	[illegible]	[illegible]	[illegible]	[illegible]	[illegible]	[illegible]	[illegible]	[illegible]	[illegible]	[illegible]	[illegible]	Total from Munster.
													Ulster:
[illegible]	[illegible]	[illegible]	[illegible]	[illegible]	[illegible]	[illegible]	[illegible]	[illegible]	[illegible]	[illegible]	[illegible]	[illegible]	[illegible]
[illegible]	[illegible]	[illegible]	[illegible]	[illegible]	[illegible]	[illegible]	[illegible]	[illegible]	[illegible]	[illegible]	[illegible]	[illegible]	Total from Ulster.
													Connaught:
[illegible]	[illegible]	[illegible]	[illegible]	[illegible]	[illegible]	[illegible]	[illegible]	[illegible]	[illegible]	[illegible]	[illegible]	[illegible]	[illegible]
[illegible]	[illegible]	[illegible]	[illegible]	[illegible]	[illegible]	[illegible]	[illegible]	[illegible]	[illegible]	[illegible]	[illegible]	[illegible]	Total from Connaught.
[illegible]	[illegible]	[illegible]	[illegible]	[illegible]	[illegible]	[illegible]	[illegible]	[illegible]	[illegible]	[illegible]	[illegible]	[illegible]	From what County not specified.
[illegible]	[illegible]	[illegible]	[illegible]	[illegible]	[illegible]	[illegible]	[illegible]	[illegible]	[illegible]	[illegible]	[illegible]	[illegible]	Total from Ireland.
													Natives of other Countries:
[illegible]	[illegible]	[illegible]	[illegible]	[illegible]	[illegible]	[illegible]	[illegible]	[illegible]	[illegible]	[illegible]	[illegible]	[illegible]	England and Wales.
[illegible]	[illegible]	[illegible]	[illegible]	[illegible]	[illegible]	[illegible]	[illegible]	[illegible]	[illegible]	[illegible]	[illegible]	[illegible]	Scotland.
[illegible]	[illegible]	[illegible]	[illegible]	[illegible]	[illegible]	[illegible]	[illegible]	[illegible]	[illegible]	[illegible]	[illegible]	[illegible]	The Continent of Europe.
[illegible]	[illegible]	[illegible]	[illegible]	[illegible]	[illegible]	[illegible]	[illegible]	[illegible]	[illegible]	[illegible]	[illegible]	[illegible]	The United States, Canada, and the West Indies.
[illegible]	[illegible]	[illegible]	[illegible]	[illegible]	[illegible]	[illegible]	[illegible]	[illegible]	[illegible]	[illegible]	[illegible]	[illegible]	Africa, Australia, and the East Indies.
[illegible]	[illegible]	[illegible]	[illegible]	[illegible]	[illegible]	[illegible]	[illegible]	[illegible]	[illegible]	[illegible]	[illegible]	[illegible]	General Total.
[illegible]		[illegible]		[illegible]		[illegible]		[illegible]		[illegible]			

—TABLE showing the Number and Ages of Persons under One Year, and One Year old and upwards, in quinquennial periods, who Emigrated from Ireland during the Year 1878; also those who stated themselves to belong to other Countries.

Carlow	[illegible]	[illegible]	[illegible]	[illegible]	[illegible]	[illegible]	[illegible]	[illegible]	[illegible]	[illegible]	[illegible]	[illegible]	[illegible]	[illegible]	[illegible]	[illegible]	[illegible]	[illegible]	[illegible]	[illegible]	[illegible]	[illegible]	[illegible]
Dublin	[illegible]	[illegible]	[illegible]	[illegible]	[illegible]	[illegible]	[illegible]	[illegible]	[illegible]	[illegible]	[illegible]	[illegible]	[illegible]	[illegible]	[illegible]	[illegible]	[illegible]	[illegible]	[illegible]	[illegible]	[illegible]	[illegible]	[illegible]
Kildare	[illegible]	[illegible]	[illegible]	[illegible]	[illegible]	[illegible]	[illegible]	[illegible]	[illegible]	[illegible]	[illegible]	[illegible]	[illegible]	[illegible]	[illegible]	[illegible]	[illegible]	[illegible]	[illegible]	[illegible]	[illegible]	[illegible]	[illegible]
Kilkenny	[illegible]	[illegible]	[illegible]	[illegible]	[illegible]	[illegible]	[illegible]	[illegible]	[illegible]	[illegible]	[illegible]	[illegible]	[illegible]	[illegible]	[illegible]	[illegible]	[illegible]	[illegible]	[illegible]	[illegible]	[illegible]	[illegible]	[illegible]
King's	[illegible]	[illegible]	[illegible]	[illegible]	[illegible]	[illegible]	[illegible]	[illegible]	[illegible]	[illegible]	[illegible]	[illegible]	[illegible]	[illegible]	[illegible]	[illegible]	[illegible]	[illegible]	[illegible]	[illegible]	[illegible]	[illegible]	[illegible]
Longford	[illegible]	[illegible]	[illegible]	[illegible]	[illegible]	[illegible]	[illegible]	[illegible]	[illegible]	[illegible]	[illegible]	[illegible]	[illegible]	[illegible]	[illegible]	[illegible]	[illegible]	[illegible]	[illegible]	[illegible]	[illegible]	[illegible]	[illegible]
Louth	[illegible]	[illegible]	[illegible]	[illegible]	[illegible]	[illegible]	[illegible]	[illegible]	[illegible]	[illegible]	[illegible]	[illegible]	[illegible]	[illegible]	[illegible]	[illegible]	[illegible]	[illegible]	[illegible]	[illegible]	[illegible]	[illegible]	[illegible]
Meath	[illegible]	[illegible]	[illegible]	[illegible]	[illegible]	[illegible]	[illegible]	[illegible]	[illegible]	[illegible]	[illegible]	[illegible]	[illegible]	[illegible]	[illegible]	[illegible]	[illegible]	[illegible]	[illegible]	[illegible]	[illegible]	[illegible]	[illegible]
Queen's	[illegible]	[illegible]	[illegible]	[illegible]	[illegible]	[illegible]	[illegible]	[illegible]	[illegible]	[illegible]	[illegible]	[illegible]	[illegible]	[illegible]	[illegible]	[illegible]	[illegible]	[illegible]	[illegible]	[illegible]	[illegible]	[illegible]	[illegible]
Westmeath	[illegible]	[illegible]	[illegible]	[illegible]	[illegible]	[illegible]	[illegible]	[illegible]	[illegible]	[illegible]	[illegible]	[illegible]	[illegible]	[illegible]	[illegible]	[illegible]	[illegible]	[illegible]	[illegible]	[illegible]	[illegible]	[illegible]	[illegible]
Wexford	[illegible]	[illegible]	[illegible]	[illegible]	[illegible]	[illegible]	[illegible]	[illegible]	[illegible]	[illegible]	[illegible]	[illegible]	[illegible]	[illegible]	[illegible]	[illegible]	[illegible]	[illegible]	[illegible]	[illegible]	[illegible]	[illegible]	[illegible]
Wicklow	[illegible]	[illegible]	[illegible]	[illegible]	[illegible]	[illegible]	[illegible]	[illegible]	[illegible]	[illegible]	[illegible]	[illegible]	[illegible]	[illegible]	[illegible]	[illegible]	[illegible]	[illegible]	[illegible]	[illegible]	[illegible]	[illegible]	[illegible]
Total of Leinster	[illegible]	[illegible]	[illegible]	[illegible]	[illegible]	[illegible]	[illegible]	[illegible]	[illegible]	[illegible]	[illegible]	[illegible]	[illegible]	[illegible]	[illegible]	[illegible]	[illegible]	[illegible]	[illegible]	[illegible]	[illegible]	[illegible]	[illegible]
Clare	[illegible]	[illegible]	[illegible]	[illegible]	[illegible]	[illegible]	[illegible]	[illegible]	[illegible]	[illegible]	[illegible]	[illegible]	[illegible]	[illegible]	[illegible]	[illegible]	[illegible]	[illegible]	[illegible]	[illegible]	[illegible]	[illegible]	[illegible]
Cork	[illegible]	[illegible]	[illegible]	[illegible]	[illegible]	[illegible]	[illegible]	[illegible]	[illegible]	[illegible]	[illegible]	[illegible]	[illegible]	[illegible]	[illegible]	[illegible]	[illegible]	[illegible]	[illegible]	[illegible]	[illegible]	[illegible]	[illegible]
Kerry	[illegible]	[illegible]	[illegible]	[illegible]	[illegible]	[illegible]	[illegible]	[illegible]	[illegible]	[illegible]	[illegible]	[illegible]	[illegible]	[illegible]	[illegible]	[illegible]	[illegible]	[illegible]	[illegible]	[illegible]	[illegible]	[illegible]	[illegible]
Limerick	[illegible]	[illegible]	[illegible]	[illegible]	[illegible]	[illegible]	[illegible]	[illegible]	[illegible]	[illegible]	[illegible]	[illegible]	[illegible]	[illegible]	[illegible]	[illegible]	[illegible]	[illegible]	[illegible]	[illegible]	[illegible]	[illegible]	[illegible]
Tipperary	[illegible]	[illegible]	[illegible]	[illegible]	[illegible]	[illegible]	[illegible]	[illegible]	[illegible]	[illegible]	[illegible]	[illegible]	[illegible]	[illegible]	[illegible]	[illegible]	[illegible]	[illegible]	[illegible]	[illegible]	[illegible]	[illegible]	[illegible]
Waterford	[illegible]	[illegible]	[illegible]	[illegible]	[illegible]	[illegible]	[illegible]	[illegible]	[illegible]	[illegible]	[illegible]	[illegible]	[illegible]	[illegible]	[illegible]	[illegible]	[illegible]	[illegible]	[illegible]	[illegible]	[illegible]	[illegible]	[illegible]
Total of Munster	[illegible]	[illegible]	[illegible]	[illegible]	[illegible]	[illegible]	[illegible]	[illegible]	[illegible]	[illegible]	[illegible]	[illegible]	[illegible]	[illegible]	[illegible]	[illegible]	[illegible]	[illegible]	[illegible]	[illegible]	[illegible]	[illegible]	[illegible]
Antrim	[illegible]	[illegible]	[illegible]	[illegible]	[illegible]	[illegible]	[illegible]	[illegible]	[illegible]	[illegible]	[illegible]	[illegible]	[illegible]	[illegible]	[illegible]	[illegible]	[illegible]	[illegible]	[illegible]	[illegible]	[illegible]	[illegible]	[illegible]
Armagh	[illegible]	[illegible]	[illegible]	[illegible]	[illegible]	[illegible]	[illegible]	[illegible]	[illegible]	[illegible]	[illegible]	[illegible]	[illegible]	[illegible]	[illegible]	[illegible]	[illegible]	[illegible]	[illegible]	[illegible]	[illegible]	[illegible]	[illegible]
Cavan	[illegible]	[illegible]	[illegible]	[illegible]	[illegible]	[illegible]	[illegible]	[illegible]	[illegible]	[illegible]	[illegible]	[illegible]	[illegible]	[illegible]	[illegible]	[illegible]	[illegible]	[illegible]	[illegible]	[illegible]	[illegible]	[illegible]	[illegible]
Donegal	[illegible]	[illegible]	[illegible]	[illegible]	[illegible]	[illegible]	[illegible]	[illegible]	[illegible]	[illegible]	[illegible]	[illegible]	[illegible]	[illegible]	[illegible]	[illegible]	[illegible]	[illegible]	[illegible]	[illegible]	[illegible]	[illegible]	[illegible]
Down	[illegible]	[illegible]	[illegible]	[illegible]	[illegible]	[illegible]	[illegible]	[illegible]	[illegible]	[illegible]	[illegible]	[illegible]	[illegible]	[illegible]	[illegible]	[illegible]	[illegible]	[illegible]	[illegible]	[illegible]	[illegible]	[illegible]	[illegible]
Fermanagh	[illegible]	[illegible]	[illegible]	[illegible]	[illegible]	[illegible]	[illegible]	[illegible]	[illegible]	[illegible]	[illegible]	[illegible]	[illegible]	[illegible]	[illegible]	[illegible]	[illegible]	[illegible]	[illegible]	[illegible]	[illegible]	[illegible]	[illegible]
Londonderry	[illegible]	[illegible]	[illegible]	[illegible]	[illegible]	[illegible]	[illegible]	[illegible]	[illegible]	[illegible]	[illegible]	[illegible]	[illegible]	[illegible]	[illegible]	[illegible]	[illegible]	[illegible]	[illegible]	[illegible]	[illegible]	[illegible]	[illegible]
Monaghan	[illegible]	[illegible]	[illegible]	[illegible]	[illegible]	[illegible]	[illegible]	[illegible]	[illegible]	[illegible]	[illegible]	[illegible]	[illegible]	[illegible]	[illegible]	[illegible]	[illegible]	[illegible]	[illegible]	[illegible]	[illegible]	[illegible]	[illegible]
Tyrone	[illegible]	[illegible]	[illegible]	[illegible]	[illegible]	[illegible]	[illegible]	[illegible]	[illegible]	[illegible]	[illegible]	[illegible]	[illegible]	[illegible]	[illegible]	[illegible]	[illegible]	[illegible]	[illegible]	[illegible]	[illegible]	[illegible]	[illegible]
Total of Ulster	[illegible]	[illegible]	[illegible]	[illegible]	[illegible]	[illegible]	[illegible]	[illegible]	[illegible]	[illegible]	[illegible]	[illegible]	[illegible]	[illegible]	[illegible]	[illegible]	[illegible]	[illegible]	[illegible]	[illegible]	[illegible]	[illegible]	[illegible]
Galway	[illegible]	[illegible]	[illegible]	[illegible]	[illegible]	[illegible]	[illegible]	[illegible]	[illegible]	[illegible]	[illegible]	[illegible]	[illegible]	[illegible]	[illegible]	[illegible]	[illegible]	[illegible]	[illegible]	[illegible]	[illegible]	[illegible]	[illegible]
Leitrim	[illegible]	[illegible]	[illegible]	[illegible]	[illegible]	[illegible]	[illegible]	[illegible]	[illegible]	[illegible]	[illegible]	[illegible]	[illegible]	[illegible]	[illegible]	[illegible]	[illegible]	[illegible]	[illegible]	[illegible]	[illegible]	[illegible]	[illegible]
Mayo	[illegible]	[illegible]	[illegible]	[illegible]	[illegible]	[illegible]	[illegible]	[illegible]	[illegible]	[illegible]	[illegible]	[illegible]	[illegible]	[illegible]	[illegible]	[illegible]	[illegible]	[illegible]	[illegible]	[illegible]	[illegible]	[illegible]	[illegible]
Roscommon	[illegible]	[illegible]	[illegible]	[illegible]	[illegible]	[illegible]	[illegible]	[illegible]	[illegible]	[illegible]	[illegible]	[illegible]	[illegible]	[illegible]	[illegible]	[illegible]	[illegible]	[illegible]	[illegible]	[illegible]	[illegible]	[illegible]	[illegible]
Sligo	[illegible]	[illegible]	[illegible]	[illegible]	[illegible]	[illegible]	[illegible]	[illegible]	[illegible]	[illegible]	[illegible]	[illegible]	[illegible]	[illegible]	[illegible]	[illegible]	[illegible]	[illegible]	[illegible]	[illegible]	[illegible]	[illegible]	[illegible]
Total of Connaught	[illegible]	[illegible]	[illegible]	[illegible]	[illegible]	[illegible]	[illegible]	[illegible]	[illegible]	[illegible]	[illegible]	[illegible]	[illegible]	[illegible]	[illegible]	[illegible]	[illegible]	[illegible]	[illegible]	[illegible]	[illegible]	[illegible]	[illegible]
[illegible]	[illegible]	[illegible]	[illegible]	[illegible]	[illegible]	[illegible]	[illegible]	[illegible]	[illegible]	[illegible]	[illegible]	[illegible]	[illegible]	[illegible]	[illegible]	[illegible]	[illegible]	[illegible]	[illegible]	[illegible]	[illegible]	[illegible]	[illegible]
Total from Ireland	[illegible]	[illegible]	[illegible]	[illegible]	[illegible]	[illegible]	[illegible]	[illegible]	[illegible]	[illegible]	[illegible]	[illegible]	[illegible]	[illegible]	[illegible]	[illegible]	[illegible]	[illegible]	[illegible]	[illegible]	[illegible]	[illegible]	[illegible]
[illegible]																							
[illegible]	[illegible]	[illegible]	[illegible]	[illegible]	[illegible]	[illegible]	[illegible]	[illegible]	[illegible]	[illegible]	[illegible]	[illegible]	[illegible]	[illegible]	[illegible]	[illegible]	[illegible]	[illegible]	[illegible]	[illegible]	[illegible]	[illegible]	[illegible]
England	[illegible]	[illegible]	[illegible]	[illegible]	[illegible]	[illegible]	[illegible]	[illegible]	[illegible]	[illegible]	[illegible]	[illegible]	[illegible]	[illegible]	[illegible]	[illegible]	[illegible]	[illegible]	[illegible]	[illegible]	[illegible]	[illegible]	[illegible]
The Continent of Europe	[illegible]	[illegible]	[illegible]	[illegible]	[illegible]	[illegible]	[illegible]	[illegible]	[illegible]	[illegible]	[illegible]	[illegible]	[illegible]	[illegible]	[illegible]	[illegible]	[illegible]	[illegible]	[illegible]	[illegible]	[illegible]	[illegible]	[illegible]
[illegible]	[illegible]	[illegible]	[illegible]	[illegible]	[illegible]	[illegible]	[illegible]	[illegible]	[illegible]	[illegible]	[illegible]	[illegible]	[illegible]	[illegible]	[illegible]	[illegible]	[illegible]	[illegible]	[illegible]	[illegible]	[illegible]	[illegible]	[illegible]
[illegible]	[illegible]	[illegible]	[illegible]	[illegible]	[illegible]	[illegible]	[illegible]	[illegible]	[illegible]	[illegible]	[illegible]	[illegible]	[illegible]	[illegible]	[illegible]	[illegible]	[illegible]	[illegible]	[illegible]	[illegible]	[illegible]	[illegible]	[illegible]
General Total	[illegible]	[illegible]	[illegible]	[illegible]	[illegible]	[illegible]	[illegible]	[illegible]	[illegible]	[illegible]	[illegible]	[illegible]	[illegible]	[illegible]	[illegible]	[illegible]	[illegible]	[illegible]	[illegible]	[illegible]	[illegible]	[illegible]	[illegible]

SCUTCHING MILLS.

RETURN of MILLS in Ireland constructed for SCUTCHING FLAX, showing the name of the County, Barony, Parish, and Townland, in which each Mill is respectively situated, and the Number of Weeks each Mill was at Work, from the 1st June, 1872, to the 31st May, 1873.

PROVINCE OF LEINSTER.

County.	Barony.	Parish.	Townland.	No. of Mills.	No. of Stocks and Handles in each Mill: Stocks.	Handles.	No. of Weeks at Work.
Carlow,	Carlow,	Carlow,	Carlow Town,	*1	8	6	.
			Total in Co. Carlow,	1	8	6	.
Dublin,	No Scutching Mill	in this County.		.	.	.	.
Kildare,	No Scutching Mill	in this County.		.	.	.	.
Kilkenny,	No Scutching Mill	in this County.		.	.	.	.
King's,	Clonlisk,	Kilcolman,	Rathbeg,	1	4	16	16
	"	Kinnitty,	Kilcomin,	1	6	30	.
			Total in King's Co.,	2	10	46	.
Longford,	Ardagh,	Templemichael,	Kilmacrige,	1	14	70	21
	Granard,	Columbkille,	Drumg,	1	6	16	.
	Longford,	Killashee,	Glebe,	1	12	64	20
			Total in Co. Longford,	3	32	151	.
Louth,	Dundalk, Lower,	Ballymascanlan,	Aghnaskeagh,	1	24	160	20
	"	"	Ravensdale,	1	6	80	.
	"	Carlingford,	Castletowncooley,	1	8	30	15
	"	"	Rathiddy,	1	4	80	.
	Dundalk, Upper,	Faughart,	Dungooly,	1	5	80	15
	"	Philipstown,	Philipstown,	1	16	80	80
	Ferrard,	Dunleer,	[illegible]	1	16	90	.
			Total in Co. Louth,	7	79	400	.
Meath,	Duleek, Lower,	[illegible]	Rossnaree,	1	4	16	.
	Fore,	Diamor,	[illegible]	1	2	10	.
	"	Killeagh,	Tully,	1	4	20	4
	Kells, Lower,	Kenlis,	[illegible]	1	4	25	17
	"	Moybolgue,	[illegible]	1	5	20	26
	"	Moynalty,	[illegible], Upper,	1	5	10	17
	Kells, Upper,	Kilbeg,	[illegible]	1	6	20	.
	Slane,	Brownstown,	Brownstown,	1	6	30	6
			Total in Co. Meath,	8	41	201	.
Queen's,	Portnahinch,	Coolbanagher,	Ballytilliam,	1	2	8	.
	Tinnahinch,	Rosenallis,	Townparks,	1	12	60	16
			Total in Queen's Co.,	2	14	68	.
Westmeath	Fore,	St. Feighins,	Barbavilla Demesne,	1	4	21	.
	Moygoish,	C. T. Kinkelan,	[illegible]	1	4	20	26
			Total in Co. Westmeath,	2	8	41	.
Wexford,	Scarawalsh,	Templeshanbo,	Ballynaslaney,	1	2	10	6
	Shelbourne,	Killesk,	Kilmannock,	1	4	20	.
	"	Rathroe,	Haggard,	1	4	20	20
	Shelmaliere, West,	Clongeen,	Loughnageer,	1	6	30	.
			Total in Co. Wexford,	4	16	80	.
Wicklow,	No Scutching Mill	in this County.		.	.	.	.
			TOTAL IN THE PROVINCE OF LEINSTER,	29	208	993	.

* Barry's Steam Power.

RETURN of MILLS in Ireland constructed for SCUTCHING FLAX—continued.

PROVINCE OF MUNSTER.

County.	Barony.	Parish.	Townland.	No. of Mills.	No. of Stocks and Persons at work daily: Stocks.	Handlers.	No. of Weeks at Work.
Clare,	Tulla, Upper,	Tomgraney,	Raheen,	1	3	19	29
	"	Tulla,	Kiltanon,	1	10	50	4
			Total in Co. Clare,	2	13	69	.
Cork,	Barrymore,	Ballinaraneak,	Ballyraugh, Lower,	1	8	40	16
	Carbery, E., E.D.,	Ballymoney,	Derrigra,	1	8	15	.
		Kilgarriff,	Tawnies, Lower,	1	18	77	34
	Carbery, E., W.D.,	Castleventry,	Inchinattin,	1	4	20	24
	"	Fanlobbus,	Darkwood,	1	4	25	17
	"	Kilmacabea,	Carrow, South,	1	8	40	16
	"	Kinneigh,	Castlelands,	1	6	35	40
	"	Ross,	Maulnageragh,	1	6	24	12
	"	"	Rossmore, N.,	1	12	62	20
	Carbery, W., E.D.,	Abbeystrowry,	Gortnamona,	1	6	30	12
	"	"	Kilcoe,	1	5	30	16
	"	"	Rossagh,	1	8	40	16
	"	Drumdaleague,	Rossmohalla,	1	6	36	.
	Condons & Clangibbon,	Fertiby,	Oak Ross Mountain,	1	6	35	16
	"	Macroney,	Ballough, West,	1	8	30	47
	Cork,	Carrigaline,	Ballybrack,	1	17	55	28
	"	St. Anne's, Shandon	Kilbegg,	1	12	60	30
	Duhallow,	Clonfert,	Meenybeg,	1	4	24	15
	"	Kilshannig,	Gortroe,	1	6	28	17
	Fermoy,	Ballyhooly,	Gortroche,	1	6	30	30
	Ibane & Barryroe,	Kilkerran,	Knocks,	1	8	40	9
	Muskerry, East,	Donaghmore,	Ooldstown,	1	2	6	8
	Orrery & Kilmore,	Ballyclogh,	Ballyclogh,	1	2	9	.
			Total in Co. Cork,	23	163	829	.
Kerry,	Corkaguiny,	Stradbally,	Knockaneroe,	1	4	20	.
	Trughanacmy,	Ratass,	Ballyvelly,	1	8	40	47
			Total in Co. Kerry,	2	12	60	.
Limerick,	No Scutching Mill	in this County.		.	.	.	.
Tipperary,	Eliogarty,	Ballymurreen,	Parkstown,	1	5	30	6
	Iffa and Offa, East,	Carrick,	Townparks,	1	7	36	.
	Iffa and Offa, West,	Shanrahan,	Clogheen Market,	1	4	8	.
	Ikerrin,	Corbally,	Birdgrove,	1	12	60	45
	Ormond, Lower,	Ardcrony,	Mountisland,	1	8	6	6
			Total in Co. Tipperary,	5	31	135	.
Waterford,	Coshmore and Coshbride,	Lismore & Mocollop,	Castlelands,	1	4	20	.
			Total in Co. Waterford,	1	4	20	.
			TOTAL IN PROVINCE OF MUNSTER,	33	223	1,142	.

RETURN of MILLS in Ireland constructed for SCUTCHING FLAX—continued.

PROVINCE OF ULSTER.

County.	Barony.	Parish.	Townland.	No. of Mills.	No. of Stocks and Handles in each Mill. Stocks.	Handles.	No. of Weeks at Work.
ANTRIM.	Antrim, Lower,	Ballyclug,	Ballybeed,	1	12	60	.
	"	"	Ballymarlagh,	1	6	30	46
	"	Connor,	Kildrum,	1	6	30	15
	"	Glenwhirry,	Jockey's Quarter,	1	11	44	16
	"	Racavan,	Aghnadore,	1	6	30	18
	"	"	Bally[illegible],	1	6	30	17
	"	"	Ditto,	1	6	30	16
	"	"	Ditto,	1	6	40	.
	"	"	Broughshane, Upper,	1	5	30	30
	"	"	Ditto,	1	17	102	7
	"	"	Craveenery,	1	4	30	.
	"	"	Lisnamurrikin,	1	6	30	24
	"	"	[illegible],	1	5	30	6
	"	"	Ditto,	1	4	30	.
	"	Skerry,	Brockagh,	1	6	30	.
	"	"	Cleggan,	1	6	30	.
	"	"	Killygore,	1	4	30	6
	"	"	Kildally,	1	4	30	.
	"	"	Knockboy,	1	5	30	12
	"	"	Loughconnelly,	1	4	30	10
	Antrim, Upper,	Ballycor,	Ballyboley,	1	6	30	16
	"	"	Ballygowan,	1	9	42	18
	"	"	Ditto,	1	4	30	6
	"	Doagh Grange,	Coggrey,	1	8	40	4
	"	Donegore,	Ballyrea,	1	6	30	28
	"	"	Ballyrea,	1	9	42	30
	"	"	Drumagorgan,	1	6	30	40
	"	Kilbride,	Ballywee,	1	6	30	24
	"	"	Drumadarragh,	1	9	44	17
	"	"	Moneyside,	1	6	30	22
	"	Nilteen Grange,	Moyadam,	1	5	30	24
	"	"	Ditto,	1	4	30	.
	"	"	Rathbeg,	1	5	22	30
	"	Rashee,	Rashee,	1	9	42	.
	Belfast, Lower,	Ballymore,	Straid,	1	3	18	28
	"	"	Ditto,	1	4	20	28
	"	Carnmoney,	Dunanney,	1	6	30	30
	"	"	Glengormly,	1	8	48	.
	"	Glynn,	Ballylume,	1	6	30	52
	"	"	Glynn,	1	4	30	30
	"	Raloo,	Ballay,	1	.	.	.
	"	"	Terragh,	1	6	30	16
	"	Templepatrick,	Craigarogan,	1	6	28	30
	"	"	Kilgreel,	1	14	90	35
	"	"	Molusk, Grange of,	1	6	30	17
	Belfast, Upper,	Derryaghy,	Derryaghy,	1	18	60	18
	"	"	Ditto,	1	12	60	.
	"	Templepatrick,	Cloghanduff,	1	6	30	18
	"	"	Killaney,	1	4	30	16
	Cary,	Armoy,	Middlemoore,	1	17	60	18
	"	"	Park,	1	6	30	8
	"	Ballintoy,	Ballinlea, Lower,	1	5	50	6
	"	"	Currysheskin,	1	6	31	3
	"	Billy,	Cloghcor, North,	1	6	35	.
	"	"	Magheraboy or [illegible],	1	6	32	.
	"	"	Moycraig (Hamilton),	1	6	30	12
	"	Culfeightrin,	Ballypatrick,	1	8	40	12
	"	"	Broughanlea,	1	8	36	22
	"	"	Drumavoley,	1	5	35	17
	"	Grange of Drumtullagh,	Moneyside,	1	8	40	14
	"	Ramoan,	Moyarget, Lower,	1	7	30	8
	Dunluce, Lower,	Ballyrashane,	Lisnablo,	1	9	31	12
	"	Billy,	Ballyness,	1	9	11	16
	"	Derrykeighan,	Clontymullan,	1	6	40	6
	"	"	Dervock,	1	6	36	16
	"	"	Knockanboy,	1	4	24	14
	"	"	Lisconnan,	1	9	14	7
	"	"	Mullaghduff,	1	6	38	12
	"	Dunluce,	Ballaghmore or [illegible],	1	6	30	20
	"	"	Ballytober,	1	6	36	30
	"	"	Ballyclogh, North,	1	6	30	25

RETURN of MILLS in Ireland constructed for SCUTCHING FLAX—continued.

PROVINCE OF ULSTER—continued.

County.	Barony.	Parish.	Townland.	No. of Mills.	No. of Stocks and Handles in each Mill: Stocks.	Handles.	No. of Weeks at Work.
	Dunluce, Upper,	Ballymoney,	Coldagh,	1	8	40	30
	"	"	[illegible], Upper,	1	4	24	28
	"	"	Killyrammer,	1	6	30	18
	"	"	Stranocum,	1	16	30	12
	"	"	Topp, Lower,	1	8	40	18
	"	Killagan,	Dromadarragh,	1	8	40	.
	"	Loughguile,	Ballyreagh, Lower,	1	4	24	30
	"	"	Ditto,	1	6	30	12
	"	"	Ballymagrabel,	1	8	6	26
	"	"	Ballyportery, North,	1	6	30	30
	"	"	Ditto,	1	4	20	.
	"	"	Ballyportery, South,	1	8	25	14
	"	"	Cloughfinnan, West,	1	4	20	.
	"	"	Corkey, South or Little,	1	8	24	24
	"	"	Culbane,	1	6	30	12
	"	"	Ditto,	1	7	12	26
	"	"	Drumadallagh,	1	4	16	18
	"	"	Kinguriff,	1	10	30	16
	Glenarm, Lower,	Layd,	Callisnagh,	1	8	40	17
	"	"	Lubitavish,	1	4	20	18
	"	"	Skeen,	1	5	40	31
	"	"	Ditto,	1	6	50	.
	"	"	Ditto,	1	6	20	.
	"	"	Tavnaghdrissagh,	1	8	30	18
	"	Tickmacrevan,	Aughareamlagh,	1	10	40	3
	"	"	Gallanagh,	1	6	30	3
	Glenarm, Upper,	Kilwaughter,	Rory's Glen,	1	18	60	36
	Kilconway,	Craigs,	Craigs,	1	6	36	14
	"	"	Ditto,	1	5	36	8
	"	Dunaghy,	Ballyreagh,	1	2	10	16
	"	"	Cargan,	1	10	50	.
	"	"	Dunbought,	1	5	30	24
	"	"	Killyree,	1	8	15	30
	"	"	Tullaghbane,	1	6	30	8
	"	"	Ditto,	1	5	30	36
Antrim—continued.	"	Finvoy,	Slievenaghy,	1	2	4	30
	"	"	Vow,	1	5	20	13
	"	Grange of Dundermot,	Springmount,	1	6	24	15
	"	Killagan,	Clogh Mills,	1	8	48	28
	"	Loughguile,	Carrowcroagh,	1	4	15	36
	"	Rasharkin,	Ardicur,	1	6	36	36
	"	"	Ditto,	1	2	12	26
	"	"	Ballydonnelly,	1	10	60	30
	"	"	Gortereghy,	1	6	16	21
	"	"	Killycreen,	1	5	30	13
	"	"	Killydonnelly,	1	6	35	14
	"	"	Magheraboy,	1	4	30	10
	"	"	Ditto,	1	4	24	11
	"	"	Ditto,	1	4	24	10
	Massereene, Lower,	Killead,	Ballymather, Lower,	1	6	30	14
	"	"	Ballyrobin,	1	4	30	.
	"	"	Scaddhavern,	1	4	30	18
	Massereene, Upper,	Ballinderry,	Ballinderry,	1	18	60	1
	"	Glenavy,	Edenturcher,	1	8	40	8
	"	Magheragall,	Moneybroom,	1	18	60	.
	"	Tullyrusk,	Dundrod,	1	6	30	4
	Toome, Lower,	Ahoghill,	Ballyloughan,	1	5	25	4
	"	"	Ballylustrale,	1	4	30	23
	"	"	Cardonaghy,	1	6	35	16
	"	"	Carnearney,	1	6	30	25
	"	"	Glenhugh,	1	7	25	24
	"	"	Leymore,	1	10	50	17
	"	Craigs,	Drumramer,	1	12	72	10
	"	"	Moylarg,	1	6	30	.
	"	Kirkinriola,	Ballygarvey,	1	8	40	26
	"	"	Cardies,	1	4	30	16
	"	Portglenone,	Gortgole,	1	5	10	35
	"	"	Killycoogan,	1	3	19	8
	"	"	Ditto,	1	3	10	18
	"	"	Killygarn,	1	4	20	12
	"	"	Ditto,	1	4	30	12

RETURN of MILLS in Ireland constructed for SCUTCHING FLAX—continued.

PROVINCE OF ULSTER—continued.

County.	Barony.	Parish.	Townland.	No. of Mills.	No. of Stocks and Handles in each Mill. Stocks.	Handles.	No. of Weeks at Work.
Antrim—continued.	Toome, Lower,	Portglenone,	Tullynahinion,	1	3	12	20
	Toome, Upper,	Ahoghill,	Straid,	1	6	30	13
	"	Antrim,	Tullyreaghgirt,	1	6	48	10
	"	Ballymullen Grange.	Grange Park,	1	14	70	36
	"	"	Mill Quarter,	1	4	60	18
	"	Drummaul,	Aghaboy,	1	10	60	16
	"	"	Ditto,	1	6	30	.
	"	"	Ballygrooby,	1	12	60	12
	"	"	Ditto,	1	2	10	3
	"	"	Caddy,	1	6	30	20
	"	Duneane,	Artlone,	1	12	50	16
	"	"	Ballymatoskerry,	1	6	30	.
	"	"	Creggan,	1	6	30	24
	"	"	Derryhollagh,	1	10	60	12
	"	"	Moneynick,	1	12	60	36
			Total in Co. Antrim,	127	994	3,164	.
Armagh,	Armagh,	Armagh,	Corporation,	1	12	60	.
	"	Derrynoose,	Drumacanver,	1	8	32	16
	"	Eglish,	Ballaghy,	1	6	30	7
	"	Keady,	Corkley,	1	12	60	13
	"	"	Dundrum,	1	8	40	10
	"	Lisnadill,	Lisbanoe,	1	17	60	.
	"	Tynan,	Balteagh,	1	18½	60	19
	"	"	Derryhaw,	1	8	40	21
	"	"	Ditto,	1	4	30	28
	"	"	Ditto,	1	4	30	20
	"	"	Drumhillery,	1	6	24	18
	"	"	Ditto,	1	6	24	16
	"	"	Ditto,	1	4	16	12
	Fews, Lower,	Kilclooney,	Ballylane,	1	6	30	18
	"	"	Ditto,	1	6	48	18
	"	"	Cladymore,	1	6	30	16
	"	"	Cordrummond,	1	8	40	9
	"	"	Edenykennedy,	1	5	30	12
	"	"	Kilmacrah,	1	6	30	6
	"	"	Lisnagat,	1	2	4	1
	"	"	Seaboughan,	1	6	20	8
	"	Lisnadill,	Belleek,	1	5	12	20
	"	"	Ballybrolly,	1	12	60	16
	"	"	Ballymacnab,	1	8	40	16
	"	"	Ballynagallagh,	1	16	80	.
	"	"	Kildeen,	1	6	24	12
	"	"	Tandragee,	1	6	30	16
	"	Loughgilly,	Drumgraw,	1	12	60	24
	"	"	Ditto,	1	10	40	6
	"	Mullaghbrack,	Ballyneary,	1	8	30	.
	"	"	Ditto,	1	4	28	1
	"	"	Brychdan,	1	8	40	4
	"	"	Drumeachan,	1	14	70	4
	"	"	Lurgaboy,	1	4	20	4
	Fews, Upper,	Ballymyre,	Corlat,	1	6	30	14
	"	"	Lurgana,	1	12	60	14
	"	Creggan,	Glassdrummond,	1	12	60	18
	"	"	Ditto,	1	14	70	20
	"	"	Tullydonnell (O'Callaghan),	1	12	60	20
	"	Newtownhamilton,	Cornaclare,	1	6	30	17
	"	"	Drumcheenanagh,	1	14	70	17
	"	"	Tullyvallen,	1	12	60	15
	"	"	Ditto,	1	6	30	14
	"	"	Ditto,	1	6	30	20
	Oneilland, East,	Seagoe,	Ballynaghy,	1	12	48	3
	"	"	Levaghery,	1	16	80	.
	Oneilland, West,	Clonfeacle,	Derryscollop,	1	10	50	6
	"	Drumcree,	Annahugh,	1	12	60	.
	"	"	Corcreevy,	1	12	60	20

Returns of Mills in Ireland employed for Scutching Flax—continued.

PROVINCE OF ULSTER—continued.

County.	Barony.	Parish.	Townland.	No. of Mills.	No. of Stocks and Handles in each Mill: Stocks.	Handles.	No. of Weeks at Work.
Armagh—continued.	Oneilland, West,	Drumcree,	Corcullentragh-more,	1	12	60	.
	"	"	Ditto,	1	8	40	.
	"	"	Drumannagh,	1	22	110	.
	"	"	Drumnakelly,	1	4	20	.
	"	Grange,	Drumart,	1	10	50	7
	"	Kilmore,	Aghory,	1	8	40	.
	"	"	Annaragh,	1	14	60	10
	"	"	Ballybreagh,	1	10	50	.
	"	"	Ballyhagan,	1	6	30	.
	"	"	Ditto,	1	8	30	1
	"	"	Ditto,	1	8	30	1
	"	"	Cavanacaw,	1	8	40	.
	"	"	Rich Hill,	1	12	60	.
	"	"	Rockmacreeny,	1	6	30	2
	"	"	Ditto,	1	6	30	3
	"	Loughgall,	Ballygasey,	1	10	50	.
	"	"	Ditto,	1	6	30	.
	"	Mullaghbrack,	Marlacoo-more,	1	6	30	.
	"	"	Shanecrackan-beg,	1	10	50	6
	"	"	Shanecrackan-more,	1	8	40	12
	"	Tartaraghan,	Cranagill,	1	8	40	1
	Orior, Lower,	Ballymore,	Ballyshiel-beg,	1	6	30	.
	"	"	Ballyshiel-more,	1	8	40	8
	"	"	Clare,	1	6	30	4
	"	"	Ditto,	1	8	40	.
	"	"	Corlust,	1	6	35	.
	"	"	Demone,	1	10	50	8
	"	"	[illegible]	1	8	40	.
	"	"	Tullyraccan,	1	6	30	12
	"	"	Ditto,	1	6	30	.
	"	Kilclooney,	Derrycughan,	1	6	30	4
	"	"	Ditto,	1	6	30	.
	"	Kilmore,	Lisavague,	1	4	20	.
	"	Loughgilly,	Ballydogherty,	1	6	35	16
	"	"	Corrinare,	1	4	20	5
	"	"	Drakey,	1	4	20	12
	"	"	Keady-beg,	1	12	60	.
	"	"	Ditto,	1	4	20	10
	"	"	Ditto,	1	6	30	12
	"	"	Keady-more,	1	6	30	5
	"	"	Kilcon,	1	7	35	6
	"	"	Killyreavy, Upper,	1	6	30	3
	"	"	Lisnalee,	1	6	30	6
	"	"	Mountnorris,	1	8	40	10
	"	"	Mullaghmore,	1	6	30	4
	Orior, Upper,	Forkhill,	Ballykeel,	1	8	40	18
	"	"	Carrigans,	1	8	40	12
	"	"	Shanroe,	1	10	40	18
	"	"	Shean,	1	12	60	26
	"	"	Ditto,	1	8	40	23
	"	Killevy,	Clogharevagh,	1	9	45	.
	"	"	Clonlum,	1	6	30	12
	"	"	Crean,	1	4	20	.
	"	"	Ditto,	1	6	30	12
	"	"	Goragh,	1	8	40	.
	"	"	Latt,	1	8	40	9
	"	"	Ditto,	1	8	40	.
	"	"	Lislea,	1	12	60	.
	"	"	Ditto,	1	4	20	.
	"	"	Mullaghglass,	1	12	60	20
	"	Loughgilly,	Carrickananny,	1	6	30	20
	"	"	Carrickgallogly,	1	4	20	12
	"	"	Creggans, Upper,	1	6	30	16
	"	"	Drumhariff,	1	10	50	16
	"	"	Ditto,	1	6	30	25
	"	"	Drumnahuncheon,	1	4	20	6
	Tiranny,	Eglish,	Carrickaness,	1	6	30	8
	"	"	Tullymore, Etra,	1	6	30	.
	"	Tynan,	Doogary,	1	6	30	27
	"	"	Lisdonwilly,	1	17	80	.
	"	"	Tullybrick (*Hamilton*),	1	16	80	41
	"	"	Tullybrick (*Kane*),	1	8	37	15

RETURN of MILLS in Ireland constructed for SCUTCHING FLAX—*continued.*

PROVINCE OF ULSTER—*continued.*

County.	Barony.	Parish.	Townland.	No. of Mills.	No. of Stocks and Handles in each Mill.		No. of Weeks at Work.
					Stocks.	Handles.	
Armagh—*continued.*	Tiranny,	Tynan,	Tynan,	1	8	40	24
	"	"	Unshog,	1	6	30	16
			Total in Co. Armagh,	128	996	4,624	.
Cavan,	Castlerahan,	Castlerahan,	Claddagh,	1	5	25	30
	"	Crosserlough,	Derryloa,	1	4	20	12
	"	Killinkere,	Greaghadossan,	1	6	30	28
	"	Lurgan,	Murmod,	1	4	20	18
	Clankee,	Bailieborough,	Galbolie,	1	12	60	36
	"	Drumgoon,	Corcloghan,	1	8	40	17
	"	Enniskeen,	Cornagee,	1	6	30	40
	"	Knockbride,	Drumhillagh, North,	1	8	40	20
	"	"	Tullylorcan,	1	5	25	48
	"	Shercock,	Corravilla,	1	8	40	36
	"	"	Darkley,	1	5	25	18
	Clanmahon,	Ballintemple,	Lackan, Lower,	1	6	36	10
	"	Kilbride,	Pollareagh,	1	9	45	4
	"	Kilmore,	Drumcarban,	1	4	20	.
	Loughtee, Lower,	Drumlane,	Killywilly,	1	8	40	.
	Loughtee, Upper,	Kilmore,	Clarebane,	1	4	20	18
	"	Larah,	Raheelagh,	1	4	20	.
	Tullygarvey,	Annagh,	Aghadreenagh,	1	6	30	15
	"	"	Killynure,	1	10	50	12
	"	Drumgoon,	Boagh,	1	6	30	16
	"	"	Cabragh,	1	8	40	24
	"	"	Lisnagoon,	1	8	40	38
	"	Drung,	Lisboduff,	1	4	20	26
	"	Kildrumsherdan,	Coppanagh,	1	4	20	24
	"	"	Drumnagran,	1	10	50	36
	"	"	Drumsillagh,	1	4	20	15
	"	"	Killycreeny,	1	8	40	26
	"	"	Leaghin,	1	6	30	29
	Tullyhaw,	Tomregan,	Doon,	1	6	30	9
	Tullyhunco,	Killashandra,	Cloggy,	1	6	30	8
	"	"	Ditto,	1	4	20	.
	"	"	Corradarren,	1	4	20	14
	"	"	Drumnawall,	1	12	60	24
	"	"	Portaliff or Townparks,	1	12	60	4
			Total in Co. Cavan,	34	224	1,126	.
Donegal,	Banagh,	Inver,	Drumduff,	1	4	24	8
	"	"	Mountcharles,	1	6	36	12
	"	Killaghtee,	Ballyloughan,	1	4	32	28
	"	Killybegs, Lower,	Drumbaran,	1	4	15	16
	"	Killymard,	Drummeenanagh,	1	2	16	.
	"	"	Rossylougan,	1	10	50	.
	Inishowen, East,	Clonca,	Drumcarbit,	1	4	16	20
	"	Clonmany,	Clehagh,	1	6	48	.
	"	"	Fegart,	1	12	96	13
	"	Culdaff,	Aghatubrid,	1	2	14	6
	"	Donagh,	Ballylosky,	1	6	42	6
	"	"	Cashel,	1	2	10	1
	"	"	Churchland Quarters,	1	6	48	20
	"	"	Tullanree,	1	6	48	14
	"	Moville, Lower,	Bredagh Glen,	1	4	32	10
	"	"	Leckenny,	1	2	8	.
	"	Moville, Upper,	Carrowkeel,	1	4	28	12
	"	"	Clare,	1	4	24	7
	"	"	Glencrow,	1	4	28	13
	"	"	Tullynavinn,	1	6	42	17
	Inishowen, West,	Burt,	Ballyederowen,	1	4	28	6
	"	"	Ditto,	1	4	28	6
	"	"	Ditto,	1	2	15	6
	"	"	Bohullion, Lower,	1	6	36	.
	"	"	Bohullion, Upper,	1	4	32	33
	"	"	Burt Level,	1	8	52	.
	"	"	Carrowreagh,	1	4	32	13

RETURN of MILLS in Ireland constructed for SCUTCHING FLAX—continued.

PROVINCE OF ULSTER—continued.

County.	Barony.	Parish.	Townland.	No. of Mills.	No. of Scutchers and Handlers at each Mill: Scutchers.	Handlers.	No. of Weeks of Work.
Donegal—continued.	Inishowen, West,	Burt,	Drumhaggart,	1	6	64	16
	"	"	Ditto,	1	4	16	.
	"	"	Dundrean,	1	2	24	16
	"	Fahan, Lower,	Ballymacarry,	1	4	42	14
	"	"	Tullyarvan,	1	16	118	24
	"	Fahan, Upper,	Ballyraine,	1	4	80	8
	"	"	Carrowcashel,	1	6	33	16
	"	"	Crislaghmore,	1	4	43	17
	"	"	Garvary,	1	4	35	.
	"	"	Ditto,	1	5	37	24
	"	"	Ditto,	1	5	24	13
	"	"	Tievebane,	1	7	14	.
	"	Inch,	Baylet,	1	8	19	.
	"	"	Carrickanee,	1	3	17	6
	"	"	Glack or Bohullion,	1	3	19	.
	"	"	Grange,	2	5	31	4
	"	"	Moress,	1	5	21	.
	"	"	Ditto,	1	7	11	6
	"	Muff,	Carnamoyle,	1	3	6	4
	"	"	Craig,	1	4	16	.
	"	"	Drumskellan,	1	5	28	6
	"	"	Ditto,	1	4	11	4
	"	"	Ditto,	1	5	11	6
	"	"	Three Trees,	1	4	28	9
	"	"	Ditto,	1	4	28	10
	"	"	Turn,	1	5	14	6
	Kilmacrenan,	Aghanunshin,	Ballymaleel,	1	5	43	27
	"	Aughnish,	Aughnish,	1	4	33	13
	"	"	Drumherriv,	1	4	32	20
	"	"	Glenalla,	1	6	49	10
	"	"	Glenkeery,	1	4	28	17
	"	"	Newmill,	1	4	38	7
	"	Clondahorky,	Cashelmore,	1	4	38	13
	"	"	Derryart,	1	4	43	13
	"	"	Faugher,	1	5	42	10
	"	"	Ditto,	1	6	38	12
	"	"	Kilmacloo,	1	5	24	12
	"	"	Ditto,	1	4	23	9
	"	"	Magheraroarty,	1	4	43	24
	"	Clondavaddog,	Kindrum,	1	4	32	15
	"	"	Springfield,	1	2	16	28
	"	"	Ditto,	1	8	24	.
	"	Conwal,	Ards, Little,	1	6	42	27
	"	"	Ballaghdery,	1	4	35	18
	"	"	Ballyboe, [illegible],	1	6	32	21
	"	"	Ballyboe, Lisnenan,	1	6	31	14
	"	"	Bohoolan,	1	3	24	6
	"	"	Carnamuggagh, Lower,	1	4	31	4
	"	"	Carnamuggagh,	1	4	40	9
	"	"	Ditto,	1	4	40	.
	"	"	Ditto,	1	3	27	6
	"	"	Carrick,	1	7	39	17
	"	"	Ditto,	1	8	21	.
	"	"	Ditto,	1	4	32	6
	"	"	Ditto,	1	3	27	4
	"	"	Ditto,	1	4	30	7
	"	"	Ditto,	1	3	27	16
	"	"	Clonmacrory,	1	2	24	6
	"	"	Ditto,	1	4	34	8
	"	"	Ditto,	1	7	16	8
	"	"	Drumnaveagh,	1	4	40	25
	"	"	Ditto,	1	6	40	24
	"	"	Keelogs,	1	2	27	1
	"	Killygarvan,	Gortkeagh,	1	4	32	16
	"	Kilmacrenan,	Ballyreenan, Lower,	1	4	33	14
	"	"	Ditto,	1	4	23	10
	"	"	Ditto,	1	4	30	20
	"	"	Court,	1	4	32	12
	"	"	Glasmullan,	1	4	32	10
	"	"	Killoughcarran,	1	4	33	17
	"	"	Mastragh,	1	4	40	9
	"	"	Tirargus,	1	4	27	8

RETURN of MILLS in Ireland constructed for SCUTCHING FLAX—continued.

PROVINCE OF ULSTER—continued.

County.	Barony.	Parish.	Townland.	No. of Mills.	No. of Stocks and Handles in each mill. Stocks.	Handles.	No. of Weeks at Work.
Donegal—continued.	Kilmacrenan,	Raymunterdoney,	Ballyboe,	1	6	24	21
	"	"	Ditto,	1	6	24	20
	"	"	Ditto,	1	4	30	22
	"	Tullaghobegly,	Ballyness,	1	8	24	16
	"	"	Ditto,	1	8	24	10
	"	"	Ditto	1	3	24	9
	"	"	Beltany,	1	3	16	.
	"	"	Calhame,	1	8	24	15
	"	"	Killult,	1	8	24	17
	"	Tullyfern,	Ballyconnelly,	1	4	32	11
	"	"	Black's Glen,	1	4	40	24
	"	"	Carn, Low,	2	6	48	15
	"	"	Ditto,	1	6	24	16
	"	"	Carrowkeel,	1	4	32	17
	"	"	Ditto,	1	4	32	.
	"	"	Creeslough,	1	6	24	.
	"	"	Moyle,	1	8	64	.
	"	"	Ditto,	1	6	48	20
	"	"	Tully Hall,	1	6	72	37
	"	"	Ditto,	1	6	72	1
	Raphoe,	Allsaints,	Castrues,	1	3	21	64
	"	"	Clone,	1	3	18	16
	"	"	Drumboy,	1	6	14	.
	"	"	Gortahork,	1	8	64	16
	"	"	Kildrum, Upper,	1	8	24	10
	"	"	Listrim,	1	4	20	.
	"	"	Mondoo,	1	4	21	21
	"	"	Ditto,	1	4	24	20
	"	"	Mongiboe,	1	6	32	30
	"	"	Newtowncunningham,	1	4	32	.
	"	"	Roosky,	1	6	30	.
	"	"	Tullyannan Glebe,	1	3	14	.
	"	"	Lane,	1	3	14	.
	"	Clonleigh,	Ballylast,	1	4	24	32
	"	"	Ballymacruster,	1	4	32	20
	"	"	Killynaught,	1	10	80	25
	"	"	Mullanveagh,	1	6	48	21
	"	"	Mayleagh,	1	8	64	30
	"	"	Stry Leros,	1	4	32	35
	"	"	Springhill,	1	3	16	4
	"	Convoy,	Aughagaslin,	1	3	16	35
	"	"	Ditto,	1	4	32	22
	"	"	Ditto,	1	3	16	30
	"	"	Drumgumberland,	1	6	48	25
	"	"	Drumnacross,	1	4	32	25
	"	"	Gobnascale,	1	6	48	25
	"	"	Letterusser,	1	8	21	.
	"	"	Magheracoppa,	1	2	16	24
	"	"	Ditto,	1	4	32	27
	"	"	Milltown,	1	6	48	30
	"	"	Ditto,	1	6	48	25
	"	Convoy,	Drumenaught,	1	4	35	14
	"	"	Milltown,	1	4	40	25
	"	Donaghmore,	Ballygeengan,	1	1	10	.
	"	"	Carn,	1	4	29	16
	"	"	Carricknahorna,	1	12	80	20
	"	"	Carricklewhear,	1	8	64	35
	"	"	Ditto,	1	2	16	24
	"	"	Ditto,	1	2	16	10
	"	"	Carn, Upper,	1	6	48	25
	"	"	Cloghard,	1	6	30	72
	"	"	Corrabrie,	1	4	32	70
	"	"	Drumbar,	1	6	48	70
	"	"	Drumeeragh,	1	12	96	15
	"	"	Garvagh,	1	2	16	23
	"	"	Gortinaneck,	1	3	24	9
	"	"	Killoraclan,	1	4	32	30
	"	"	Mauch,	1	4	32	19
	"	"	Ditto,	1	4	32	15
	"	"	Ditto,	1	4	32	19
	"	"	Liscooly,	1	10	80	30
	"	"	Mullanboy,	1	10	80	25

RETURN of MILLS in Ireland constructed for SCUTCHING FLAX—continued.

PROVINCE OF ULSTER—continued.

County.	Barony.	Parish.	Townland.	No. of Mills.	No. of Stocks and Handles in each Mill. Stocks.	Handles.	No. of Weeks at Work.
Donegal—continued.	Raphoe,	Donaghmore,	Mullenboy,	1	6	42	1
	"	"	Navenny,	1	4	33	6
	"	"	Sessiagh (O'Neill),	1	4	33	9
	"	Killea,	Altaghaderry,	1	9	21	30
	"	"	Ditto,	1	4	22	.
	"	"	Imlick,	1	6	46	24
	"	"	Legnaduff,	1	6	42	23
	"	"	Ditto,	1	3	21	
	"	Kilteevoge,	Corvaine,	1	4	32	15
	"	"	Ditto,	1	4	32	18
	"	"	Kinnaderry,	1	6	46	12
	"	"	Welchtown,	1	8	48	18
	"	"	Ditto,	1	6	43	21
	"	Leck,	Ardagunnaky,	1	4	32	7
	"	"	Ballyboe,	1	4	32	11
	"	"	Ballyconnelly,	1	3	24	8
	"	"	Carrygally,	1	4	40	9
	"	"	Knockbrack,	1	4	32	33
	"	"	Ditto,	1	3	26	30
	"	"	Lurgy,	1	4	32	1
	"	"	Ditto,	1	3	26	33
	"	"	Pluck,	1	6	42	.
	"	"	Ditto,	1	24	160	14
	"	Raphoe,	Ballyholey, Near,	1	6	42	20
	"	"	Baltony,	1	6	64	47
	"	"	Carrickbrack,	1	4	32	24
	"	"	Cronaderry,	1	6	42	31
	"	"	Dullin,	1	4	20	.
	"	"	Kilcade,	1	6	64	40
	"	"	Magherahone,	1	4	32	27
	"	"	Milltown,	1	6	46	30
	"	"	[illegible],	1	6	48	24
	"	"	Tullydonnell, Lower,	1	4	32	1
	"	Raymoghy,	Balleeghan,	1	4	32	15
	"	"	Ditto,	1	8	64	15
	"	"	Ballyboe,	1	4	32	25
	"	"	Ballykevin,	1	3	24	19
	"	"	Carrickballydooey,	1	2	18	18
	"	"	Ditto,	1	2	16	20
	"	"	Carrickanamer,	1	2	14	20
	"	"	Drumcarn,	1	2	11	8
	"	"	Drumoghill,	1	4	32	16
	"	"	Killyverry,	1	8	24	25
	"	"	Ditto,	1	8	61	12
	"	"	Ditto,	1	4	32	12
	"	"	Kincraigy,	1	4	35	.
	"	"	Ditto,	1	4	32	8
	"	"	Milltown,	1	3	24	20
	"	"	Moneymore,	1	4	32	30
	"	"	Raymoghy,	1	4	33	30
	"	"	Rossky,	1	2	14	4
	"	"	Tinklersford,	1	3	24	.
	"	"	Tirharon,	1	3	24	10
	"	Stranorlar,	Drumboe, Lower,	1	8	46	12
	"	"	[illegible],	1	4	28	13
	"	"	Listrue,	1	4	23	8
	"	"	Stranorlar,	1	2	18	4
	"	"	Tonagun,	1	4	32	16
	"	"	[illegible],	1	4	32	12
	"	Taughboyne,	Ardagh,	1	4	29	22
	"	"	Ballyquinlan,	1	4	30	12
	"	"	Castletown,	1	6	44	22
	"	"	Cloghagarran,	1	4	32	10
	"	"	Ditto,	1	4	30	30
	"	"	Cloghfin,	1	2	14	.
	"	"	Dromore, Big,	1	4	32	.
	"	"	Ditto,	1	4	35	12
	"	"	Drumbeg,	1	4	32	8
	"	"	Drummore,	1	3	24	25
	"	"	Drumenan,	1	3	21	25
	"	"	Haw,	1	6	42	6
	"	"	Karnacally,	1	4	32	22

RETURN of MILLS in IRELAND employed for SCUTCHING FLAX—continued.

PROVINCE OF ULSTER—continued.

County.	Barony.	Parish.	Townland.	No. of Mills.	No. of Stocks and Handles in each Mill: Stocks.	Handles.	No. of Weeks at Work.
Donegal—continued.	Raphoe,	Taughboyne,	Kinnamully,	1	4	27	20
	"	"	Ditto,	1	3	21	24
	"	"	Listicall, Lower,	1	1	25	26
	"	"	Momeen,	1	5	34	16
	"	"	Treanmagh,	1	6	42	15
	"	"	Tullyowen,	1	3	24	8
	"	"	Tullyvogy,	1	6	12	20
	"	Urney,	Callane,	1	8	16	26
	"	"	Drumdeel,	1	1	30	16
	"	"	Magheryrodaghan,	1	8	16	26
	Tirhugh,	Donegal,	Clarbogbrack,	1	4	22	14
	"	"	Drumcrough,	1	4	22	13
	"	"	Drumlaght,	1	6	22	16
	"	"	Drumnacoil,	1	6	22	18
	"	Drumhome,	Ballymagrorty (Scotch),	1	4	22	9
	"	"	Killymard,	1	10	60	11
	"	"	Lurgan or Ballyraddelly,	1	10	75	12
	"	"	Moneymore,	1	8	60	14
	"	"	Mullans,	1	6	36	10
	"	"	Rath,	1	8	54	12
	"	"	Ditto,	1	4	36	12
	"	"	Trummun, East,	1	4	34	10
	"	"	Tullygallon,	1	6	30	12
	"	"	Tullybrogue or Tullybrook,	1	4	24	.
	"	"	Tullycroe,	1	4	28	8
	"	Inishmacsaint,	Ardfarn,	1	8	61	17
	"	Kilbarron,	Abbey Island,	1	6	46	28
	"	"	Abbeylands,	1	5	22	27
	"	"	Ditto,	1	6	46	.
	"	Templecarn,	Ardnaglass,	1	8	60	13
			Total in Co. Donegal,	279	1,281	8,165	.
Down,	Ards, Lower,	Bangor,	Ballymaconnell,	1	16	60	14
	"	"	Ditto,	1	3	15	16
	"	"	Ditto,	1	4	25	18
	"	"	Portavoe,	1	6	30	6
	"	Donaghadee,	Ballycopeland,	1	4	16	.
	"	"	Ditto,	1	4	20	.
	"	"	Ballymacruise,	1	17	64	20
	"	"	Craigboy,	1	5	15	20
	"	"	Ganaway,	1	16	75	20
	"	"	Two quarters of Donaghadee,	2	15	75	15
	"	Greyabbey,	Tullyboard,	1	10	40	20
	"	Newtownards,	Ballyblack,	1	12	60	9
	"	"	Bootown,	1	12	60	.
	"	"	Cunningburn,	1	18	90	9
	Ards, Upper,	Ardkeen,	Ardkeen,	1	10	50	28
	"	Ardquin,	Ballybeary,	1	4	20	.
	"	"	Ballyherly,	1	12	60	12
	"	Ballywalter,	Ballyferis,	1	2	12	.
	"	Inishargy,	Glastry,	1	22	130	.
	"	"	Kircubbin,	1	24	130	.
	"	"	Ditto,	1	12	60	24
	Castlereagh, Lower,	Bangor,	Ballymacleagh, Major,	1	8	18	10
	"	Comber,	Ballyaltikilligan,	1	6	60	11
	"	"	Ballyalloly,	1	2	15	20
	"	"	Ballygowan,	1	16	60	.
	"	"	Ballyhenry,	1	14	70	.
	"	"	Ballymagaughey,	1	6	30	12
	"	"	Ballyrickard,	1	8	18	.
	"	"	Ballystockart,	1	8	30	16
	"	"	Ballywilliam,	1	6	30	12
	"	"	Cullintraw,	1	5	14	6
	"	"	Gransha,	1	9	45	9
	"	"	Ditto,	1	6	30	16
	"	"	Ditto,	1	8	15	7
	"	"	Lisleen,	1	9	14	6
	"	"	Longlands,	1	3	15	.

RETURN of MILLS in Ireland constructed for SCUTCHING FLAX—continued.

PROVINCE OF ULSTER—continued.

County.	Barony.	Parish.	Townland.	No. of Mills.	No. of Stocks and Handles in each Mill. Stocks.	Handles.	No. of Weeks at Work.
Down—continued.	Castlereagh, Lower,	Comber,	Longlands,	1	2	12	.
	"	"	Mount Alexander,	1	12	60	.
	"	"	Ringcreevy,	1	9	45	16
	"	"	Tullyhubbert,	1	12	60	12
	"	Dundonald,	Ballyhanwood,	1	3	15	18
	"	"	Carrowreagh,	1	18	94	20
	"	"	Ditto,	1	6	25	.
	"	"	Ditto,	1	6	15	.
	"	"	Unicarval,	1	3	16	7
	"	Holywood,	Ballykeel,	1	5	24	12
	"	Killinchy,	Ballyvieghan,	1	6	13	12
	"	"	Ballygowan,	1	10	50	.
	"	"	Ravara,	1	6	24	24
	"	Kilmood,	Ballyministragh,	1	6	30	17
	"	"	Ditto,	1	9	44	18
	"	"	Ditto,	1	3	12	.
	"	"	Kilmood and Ballybunden,	1	14	60	20
	"	"	Ditto,	1	6	30	20
	"	Newtownards,	Newtownards T.,	1	14	75	10
	"	"	Ditto,	1	6	30	.
	"	"	Tullynagardy,	1	12	60	13
	Castlereagh, Upper,	Blaris,	Duneight,	1	12	60	16
	"	"	Lisnoe,	1	4	20	24
	"	Drumbo,	Ballydollaghan,	1	8	36	20
	"	"	Ballynavally,	1	4	20	14
	"	"	Cargacreevy,	1	6	28	14
	"	"	Edenderry,	1	4	16	5
	"	"	Mealough,	1	7	40	7
	"	Killaney,	Carrickmaddyroe,	1	4	20	10
	"	Killinchy,	Carrickmannon,	1	12	48	.
	"	Kilmore,	Barnamaghery,	1	4	16	6
	"	"	Carnacally,	1	4	20	.
	"	"	Creevyargon,	1	6	20	12
	"	"	Lisdoonan,	1	5	40	8
	"	"	Lisoara,	1	6	20	25
	"	"	Listooder,	1	6	22	9
	"	Knockbreda,	Ballydollaghan,	1	9	22	9
	"	"	Ballylenaghan,	1	6	40	9
	"	"	Ballymaconaghy,	1	30	180	16
	"	"	Ditto,	1	50	200	.
	"	"	Cregagh,	1	15	80	16
	"	Saintfield,	Ballyknockan,	1	18	80	6
	"	"	Bresagh,	1	16	60	6
	"	"	Ditto,	1	4	20	10
	"	"	Glasdrumman,	1	16	80	.
	Dufferin,	Killinchy,	Balloo,	1	12	68	16
	"	Killyleagh,	Corporation,	1	20	100	14
	"	"	Tullymacnous,	1	15	60	18
	Iveagh, Lower, Lower part,	Annahilt,	Ballymurphy,	1	6	30	4
	"	"	Cargycreevy,	1	4	20	6
	"	"	Cluntagh,	1	4	20	6
	"	"	Magheraconluce,	1	6	30	17
	"	Dromara,	Aughnaskeagh,	1	8	30	16
	"	"	Ditto,	1	8	30	14
	"	"	Dromara,	1	12	60	16
	"	"	Ditto,	1	6	30	.
	"	Dromore,	Ballyvicknacally,	1	22	114	26
	"	"	Ditto,	1	6	30	13
	"	"	Coolsallagh,	1	10	40	.
	"	"	Drumaknockan,	1	12	60	9
	"	"	Kinallen,	1	6	40	11
	"	"	Lappoges,	1	6	30	26
	"	Garvaghy,	Tullinisky,	1	18	90	13
	"	"	Ditto,	1	6	30	15
	Iveagh, Lower, Upper part,	Blaris,	Ravernet,	1	12	60	.
	"	Donaghcloney,	Tullycarn,	1	10	50	.
	"	Hillsborough,	[illegible],	1	14	70	9
	"	"	[illegible],	1	4	24	16
	"	Magheralin,	Drumnabreeze,	1	8	30	.
	"	"	Drumo and Drumnura,	1	15	60	16

RETURN of MILLS in Ireland constructed for SCUTCHING FLAX—continued.

PROVINCE OF ULSTER—continued.

County.	Barony.	Parish.	Townland.	No. of Mills.	No. of Stocks and Handles in each Mill. Stocks.	Handles.	No. of Weeks at Work.
Down—continued.	Iveagh, Lower, Upper part,	Magheralin,	Drumo and Drumnabreeze,	1	16	60	10
	"	"	Ditto,	1	13	60	
	"	Tullylish,	Ballymagerrick,	1	12	60	8
	"	"	Drumnascamph,	1	9	40	18
	"	"	Kernan,	1	6	30	
	"	"	Ditto,	1	6	30	11
	"	"	Knocknagore,	1	16	80	
	"	"	Ditto,	1	4	24	19
	Iveagh, Upper, Lower part,	Clonduff,	Ballyaughian,	1	8	40	6
	"	"	Ditto,	1	6	40	7
	"	"	Bally[illegible], Upper,	1	6	30	18
	"	"	Ballymaghery,	1	14	70	16
	"	"	Ballynagappoge,	1	10	60	40
	"	"	Carcullion,	1	8	30	2
	"	"	Clonmack,	1	14	70	4
	"	"	Drumnascamph,	1	10	40	2
	"	"	Kinghill,	1	13	60	4
	"	"	Leitrim,	1	6	50	8
	"	"	Lisnamulligan,	1	8	40	6
	"	Dromore,	Crossgar,	1	6	30	27
	"	"	Greenan,	1	6	30	14
	"	Drumballyroney,	Ballytrick,	1	12	60	8
	"	"	Ballynaskeagh,	1	5	30	10
	"	"	Ditto,	1	10	55	19
	"	"	Ditto,	1	4	30	10
	"	"	Drumdrenagh,	1	10	50	19
	"	"	Grallaghgreenan,	1	10	60	10
	"	"	Lackan,	1	12	60	13
	"	"	[illegible],	1	3	35	20
	"	Drumgooland,	Backaderry,	1	8	40	24
	"	"	Ballymaghlaghy,	1	16	60	16
	"	"	Ballyward,	1	4	30	8
	"	"	Ditto,	1	8	40	14
	"	"	Cloghskelt,	1	4	30	20
	"	"	Derryneill,	1	6	30	12
	"	"	Legananny,	1	6	30	19
	"	"	Leitrim,	1	4	30	20
	"	"	Magheramayo,	1	4	30	20
	"	"	Moneyslane,	1	14	65	
	"	"	Ditto,	1	12	60	17
	"	"	Slievenaboley,	1	8	40	4
	"	Garvaghy,	Balloolymore,	1	4	30	10
	"	"	Skeagh,	1	4	30	35
	"	"	Tullyorior,	1	4	15	20
	"	Kilcoo,	Ballymoney,	1	6	30	10
	"	"	Burrenreagh,	1	10	50	
	"	"	Tullyree,	1	6	30	12
	"	"	Ditto,	1	6	30	7
	"	Kilmegan,	Ballywillwill,	1	6	30	35
	"	"	Clarkill,	1	6	30	16
	"	Maghera,	Ballyrelany,	1	8	10	10
	"	"	Ditto,	1	4	10	
	"	Newry,	Shannaghan,	1	14	70	12
	"	"	Ditto,	1	16	80	20
	"	"	Ditto,	1	4	30	15
	"	"	Ditto,	1	4	30	10
	"	"	Ditto,	1	4	30	7
	Iveagh, Upper, Upper part,	Aghaderg,	Bally[illegible],	1	8	40	44
	"	"	Creevy,	1	4	30	5
	"	"	Drumsallagh,	1	6	30	16
	"	"	Glaskermore,	1	12	60	28
	"	"	Ditto,	1	10	60	25
	"	"	Greenan,	1	8	45	27
	"	"	Ditto,	1	8	40	16
	"	"	[illegible],	1	14	70	
	"	"	Scarva,	1	4	30	14
	"	Annaclone,	Ardbrin,	1	8	40	14
	"	"	Ditto,	1	12	60	18
	"	"	Cappagh,	1	6	30	20

RETURN of MILLS in Ireland constructed for SCUTCHING FLAX,—continued.

PROVINCE OF ULSTER—continued.

County.	Barony.	Parish.	Townland.	No. of Mills.	No. of Scutches and [illegible] in each Mill: [illegible]	[illegible]	No. of Weeks at Work.
Down—continued	Iveagh, Upper, Upper part,	Clonallan,	Burren,	1	12	30	12
	"	"	Ditto,	1	6	36	7
	"	"	Ditto,	1	6	36	9
	"	"	Cabragh,	1	6	36	12
	"	"	Ditto,	1	4	30	10
	"	"	Clontafleece,	1	8	30	.
	"	"	Crown,	1	4	30	20
	"	"	Ditto,	1	4	30	.
	"	"	Lurgancanty,	1	4	30	.
	"	"	Milltown,	1	10	60	17
	"	Donaghmore,	Aughin[illegible],	1	8	40	16
	"	"	Ditto,	1	6	50	.
	"	"	Ballymacaratty Beg,	1	10	30	10
	"	"	Ditto,	1	4	30	4
	"	"	Ballymacaratty More,	1	12	60	9
	"	Drumgath,	Barnmeen,	1	4	30	20
	"	"	Drumdreagh,	1	6	30	12
	"	"	Kilkarrif,	1	10	30	15
	"	"	Tullyquilly,	1	12	60	21
	"	Kilbroney,	Ballymoney,	1	4	30	16
	"	"	Newtown,	1	12	60	20
	"	Seapatrick,	Ballievy,	1	16	75	19
	"	"	Tullyconnaught,	1	4	30	20
	"	Warrenpoint,	Narrow-water,	1	12	45	15
	Kinelarty,	Kilmore,	Drumaghlis,	1	6	30	18
	"	"	Drumnaconagher,	1	4	30	21
	"	"	Ditto,	1	8	25	24
	"	"	Rademan,	1	9	20	.
	"	Loughinisland,	Drumaroad,	1	4	30	19
	"	"	Drum[illegible],	1	8	30	18
	"	"	Drum[illegible],	1	16	30	.
	"	"	Ditto,	1	11	45	17
	"	Magheradrool,	Ballymacarn, North,	1	4	30	27
	"	"	Ballymacarn, South,	1	12	30	26
	"	"	Ditto,	1	5	30	22
	"	"	Bally[illegible],	1	9	40	22
	"	"	Ditto,	1	12	60	15
	"	"	Drumaness,	1	38	150	42
	"	"	Ditto,	1	12	60	14
	"	"	Ditto,	1	5	30	21
	"	"	Magheradrool,	1	5	30	16
	"	Magherahamlet,	Ballytrim,	1	6	30	.
	"	"	Edendarriff,	1	7	55	.
	Lecale, Lower,	Ballyculter,	Ballyculter,	1	11	55	6
	"	"	Ditto,	1	4	30	.
	"	Inch,	Annacloy,	1	20	100	15
	"	Kilclief,	Kilclief,	1	12	60	7
	"	Saul,	Saul,	1	15	60	11
	Lecale, Upper,	Down,	Downpatrick Town,	1	12	60	10
	"	"	Lis[illegible],	1	4	55	17
	"	"	Magheralagan,	1	6	20	18
	Mourne,	Kilkeel,	Aughnahoory,	1	6	35	20
	"	"	Ballinran,	1	9	40	11
	"	"	Ditto,	1	6	40	11
	"	"	Ballykeel,	1	10	40	10
	"	"	Ditto,	1	6	35	16
	"	"	Bally[illegible],	1	10	30	22
	"	"	Ballymageogh,	1	9	10	16
	"	"	Carrigenagh,	1	8	40	14
	"	"	Kil[illegible],	1	9	40	21
	"	"	Leitrim,	1	4	30	16
	"	"	Tullyframe,	1	10	60	14
	Newry, Lordship of,	Newry,	Carnmeen,	1	6	40	24
	"	"	Ditto,	1	9	40	.
	"	"	Castle Enigan,	1	6	30	14
	"	"	Ditto,	1	10	40	1
	"	"	Damolly,	1	27	110	.
	"	"	Derryleckagh,	1	12	60	.
	"	"	Desart,	1	6	30	11
	"	"	Finnard,	1	12	30	20
	"	"	Lisduff,	1	6	60	16

RETURN of MILLS in Ireland constructed for Scutching Flax—continued.

PROVINCE OF ULSTER—continued.

County.	Barony.	Parish.	Townland.	No. of Mills.	No. of Stocks and Handles in each Mill: Stocks.	Handles.	No. of Weeks at Work.
Down—continued.	Newry, Lordship of,	Newry,	Loughorne,	1	10	40	-
	„	„	[illegible]	1	4	20	6
	„	„	Ditto,	1	6	30	6
			Total in Co. Down,	849	2,145	10,079	-
Fermanagh,	Clanawley,	Killesher,	Tully,	1	8	40	30
	Clankelly,	Clones,	[illegible]	1	2	10	4
	„	„	[illegible]	1	6	36	17
	„	Drummully,	[illegible]	1	2	10	-
	„	Galloon,	Derragh,	1	9	42	28
	Coole,	„	M'Dade,	1	6	30	26
	Lurg,	Drumkeeran,	[illegible]	1	18	126	20
	„	Magheraculmoney,	[illegible]	1	4	20	-
	„	„	[illegible]	1	6	36	15
	„	„	Largy,	1	4	14	30
	„	Templecarn,	[illegible]	1	4	32	18
	Magheraboy,	Inishmacsaint,	Derrygonnelly,	1	6	30	-
	„	„	[illegible]	1	4	30	18
	Magherastephana,	Aghalurcher,	[illegible]	1	8	40	31
	„	„	[illegible]	1	6	30	24
	„	„	[illegible]	1	6	36	20
	„	„	Tully, North,	1	8	25	17
	„	Aghavea,	[illegible]	1	6	30	18
	„	„	[illegible]	1	16	80	22
	„	„	[illegible]	1	8	40	16
	Tirkennedy,	Derryvullan,	Coppy,	1	6	26	28
	„	Enniskillen,	[illegible]	1	6	30	24
	„	„	[illegible]	1	4	20	22
	„	„	[illegible]	1	8	[illegible]	12
	„	„	[illegible]	1	7	31	15
	„	Magheracross,	Ballinamallard,	1	4	28	18
	„	„	[illegible]	1	7	41	12
	„	„	Ditto,	1	8	44	18
			Total in Co. Fermanagh,	[illegible]	[illegible]	1,007	-
Londonderry,	Coleraine,	Aghadowey,	[illegible]	1	4	16	10
	„	„	[illegible]	1	8	40	22
	„	„	[illegible]	1	4	24	24
	„	„	[illegible]	1	4	24	24
	„	„	[illegible]	1	4	24	14
	„	„	[illegible]	1	10	40	19
	„	„	Ditto,	1	6	24	14
	„	„	[illegible]	1	18	72	27
	„	„	[illegible]	1	6	28	24
	„	„	[illegible]	1	4	24	16
	„	Desertoghill,	[illegible]	1	6	28	20
	„	„	[illegible]	1	4	24	24
	„	„	[illegible]	1	4	24	22
	„	„	[illegible]	1	6	30	20
	„	„	[illegible]	1	4	20	8
	„	Dunboe,	[illegible]	1	6	24	12
	„	„	Articlave, Lower,	1	6	28	6
	„	„	Ditto,	1	2	12	-
	„	„	Articlave, Upper,	1	8	24	12
	„	„	[illegible]	1	6	30	18
	„	„	[illegible]	1	2	12	12
	„	„	[illegible]	1	6	30	16
	„	Errigal,	[illegible]	1	4	24	24
	„	„	[illegible]	1	11	55	30
	„	„	Ditto,	1	4	16	16
	„	„	Ditto,	1	4	16	16
	„	Macosquin,	[illegible]	1	4	24	28
	„	„	[illegible], Lower,	1	4	24	28
	„	„	[illegible]	1	6	26	21
	„	„	[illegible]	1	4	24	30

RETURN of MILLS in Ireland constructed for SCUTCHING FLAX—continued.

PROVINCE OF ULSTER—continued.

County.	Barony.	Parish.	Townland.	No. of Mills.	No. of Stocks and Handles in each Mill. Stocks.	Handles.	No. of Weeks at Work.
Londonderry, continued.	Coleraine,	Macosquin,	Macosquin,	1	6	26	31
	Keenaght,	Balteagh,	Ardmore,	1	6	48	4
	"	"	Drumagosker,	1	6	36	20
	"	"	Ditto,	1	4	24	22
	"	"	Drumagarvanny, Lower,	1	4	24	40
	"	"	Ditto,	1	6	36	40
	"	"	Drumsurn, Upper,	1	3	18	[illegible]
	"	"	Maine, North,	1	6	36	6
	"	"	Terrydremont, North,	1	15	96	30
	"	"	Ditto,	1	7	46	30
	"	Banagher,	Aughlish,	1	4	32	14
	"	"	Carnanbane,	1	6	48	34
	"	"	Derrychrier,	1	[illegible]	42	30
	"	"	Fincarn,	1	3	18	12
	"	"	Gallany,	1	3	16	30
	"	"	Ditto,	1	3	15	12
	"	"	Magheramore,	1	10	60	8
	"	Bovevagh,	Ardinarive,	1	4	24	31
	"	"	Ballyharigan,	1	6	30	11
	"	"	Muldonagh,	1	4	22	16
	"	"	Straw,	1	6	36	23
	"	Carrick,	Ballyduerrog,	1	6	36	6
	"	"	Ditto,	1	4	24	25
	"	"	Ballyness,	1	4	21	30
	"	Drumachose,	Ballymaclanigan,	1	4	29	24
	"	"	Rokea,	1	6	35	17
	"	"	Drummond,	1	6	36	30
	"	Dungiven,	Crebarkey,	1	6	38	.
	"	"	Derryork,	1	6	36	30
	"	"	Gortgarn,	1	4	15	9
	"	"	Lackagh,	1	15	73	30
	"	"	Magheroskey,	1	5	36	30
	"	"	Ovil,	1	12	70	8
	"	"	Ditto,	1	5	42	38
	"	"	Tamniarin,	1	4	24	18
	"	"	Turmeel,	1	6	35	12
	"	Tamlaght Finlagan,	Ballyhenry, West,	1	11	64	19
	"	"	Drumrane,	1	6	36	17
	"	"	Ditto,	1	4	24	10
	"	"	Glasvey,	1	6	46	14
	"	"	Ditto,	1	4	36	.
	"	"	Tamlaght,	1	6	36	16
	Loughinsholin,	Arboe,	Ballygurk Beg,	1	4	24	23
	"	"	Drumenvillan,	1	5	36	33
	"	Artrea,	Ballygurk,	1	3	18	35
	"	"	Derrygarve,	1	6	30	30
	"	"	Mawillan,	1	4	24	.
	"	"	Moneymore Town,	1	6	42	40
	"	Ballynascreen,	Brackagh,	1	6	36	23
	"	"	Cavanreagh,	1	3	19	21
	"	"	Doon,	1	3	12	4
	"	"	Glengomna,	1	4	24	12
	"	"	Labby,	1	4	24	13
	"	"	Moyheeland,	1	6	35	24
	"	"	Straw,	1	4	24	30
	"	"	Ditto,	1	4	21	30
	"	Ballinderry,	Ballydonnell,	1	4	24	.
	"	"	Ballymulderg,	1	3	19	25
	"	"	Ditto,	1	3	12	17
	"	"	Ditto,	1	4	24	17
	"	Ballyscullion,	Drumanee, Lower,	1	3	19	1
	"	"	Killyberry,	1	3	12	46
	"	Derryloran,	Annahavil,	1	6	36	22
	"	"	Derrycrummy,	1	6	30	26
	"	Desertlyn,	Carndaisy,	1	3	10	.
	"	"	Carrydarragh,	1	3	6	12
	"	"	Lurgamarrow,	1	6	30	30
	"	"	Moyinsakinerry,	1	3	6	
	"	Desertmartin,	Annagh & Moneysterlin,	1	8	48	33
	"	"	Bennagh,	1	6	36	24
	"	"	Brackaghslievegallion,	1	4	24	35
	"	"	Dunmarallon,	1	6	48	17

RETURN of MILLS in Ireland constructed for SCUTCHING FLAX—continued.

PROVINCE OF ULSTER—continued.

County.	Barony.	Parish.	Townland.	No. of Mills.	No. of Stocks and Handles in each Mill: Stocks.	Handles.	No. of Weeks at Work.
Londonderry—con.	Loughinsholin,	Desertmartin,	Oaranagarvy,	1	3	18	9
	"	"	Longfield,	1	8	48	12
	"	"	Luney,	1	9	48	10
	"	"	Stranagard,	1	9	48	12
	"	Kilcronaghan,	Cloughfin,	1	6	36	20
	"	"	Coolsaragh,	1	6	36	23
	"	"	Moneyshanere,	1	6	18	23
	"	"	Tobermore,	1	3	18	23
	"	Killelagh,	Ballyknock,	1	4	24	46
	"	"	Culnagrew,	1	4	24	37
	"	"	Tirnony,	1	10	40	58
	"	"	Tullyheran,	1	3	18	20
	"	Lissan,	Ballybriest,	1	4	24	17
	"	"	Brackagh,	1	4	24	20
	"	"	Cannon,	1	3	12	17
	"	"	Derrygenard,	1	3	18	18
	"	"	Dirnan,	1	3	18	17
	"	"	Ditto,	1	3	18	19
	"	"	Drumard,	1	3	18	23
	"	"	Drummond (*Drapers*),	1	4	28	25
	"	"	Killybearn,	1	4	20	32
	"	"	Ditto,	1	4	20	23
	"	"	Knockadoo,	1	4	30	30
	"	"	Ditto,	1	2	12	24
	"	"	Lisnamorrow,	1	6	36	24
	"	"	Ditto,	1	6	36	.
	"	"	Rossmore,	1	4	21	17
	"	"	Tintagh,	1	4	24	24
	"	"	Ditto,	1	5	40	.
	"	"	Ditto,	1	3	18	24
	"	Maghera,	Ballymacilcurr,	1	2	12	20
	"	"	Crew,	1	2	12	23
	"	"	Culnady,	1	4	24	27
	"	"	Ditto,	1	1	6	23
	"	"	Ditto,	1	2	12	42
	"	"	Ditto,	1	1	6	26
	"	"	Curragh,	1	3	18	20
	"	"	Drumlamp,	1	6	36	16
	"	"	Grillagh,	1	4	40	20
	"	"	Ditto,	1	1	40	20
	"	"	Mawsagh,	1	8	75	20
	"	"	Upperland,	1	6	30	20
	"	Magherafelt,	Castle Dawson Town,	1	18	90	40
	"	"	Lorkagh,	1	4	24	22
	"	"	Magargy,	1	6	30	26
	"	"	Ditto,	1	6	30	19
	"	"	Polepatrick,	1	6	36	25
	"	"	Tully[illegible],	1	6	36	15
	"	"	Ditto,	1	12	72	20
	"	Tamlaght,	Drumard,	1	6	30	20
	"	"	Ditto,	1	4	24	.
	"	Tamlaght O'Crilly,	Inishrush,	1	6	18	17
	"	"	Moneyneagh,	1	4	24	21
	"	"	Tamnyaskey,	1	2	12	20
	"	Termoneeny,	Brough,	1	6	36	20
	"	"	Ditto,	1	6	36	16
	"	"	Cabragh,	1	11	66	.
	North-east Liberties of Coleraine,	Ballyrashane,	Kirkistown,	1	6	48	22
	"	Coleraine,	Bushill,	1	8	48	20
	"	"	Coleraine Town,	1	8	43	25
	"	"	Dullam,	1	10	30	21
	"	Kildollagh,	Fishloughan,	1	8	40	20
	"	"	Mill-loughan,	1	13	40	22
	"	"	Ditto,	1	1	10	12
	North-west Liberties of Londonderry,	Templemore,	Ballymagrorty,	1	2	18	32
	"	"	Ballynashallog,	1	6	36	6
	"	"	Coshquin,	1	5	30	.
	"	"	Ditto,	1	5	24	.
	"	"	Elagh,	1	4	25	32
	Tirkeeran,	Banagher,	Drumcovit,	1	6	44	47

Return of Mills in Ireland constructed for Scutching Flax—continued.

PROVINCE OF ULSTER—continued.

County.	Barony.	Parish.	Townland.	No. of Mills.	No. of Stocks and Handles in each Mill: Stocks.	Handles.	No. of Weeks at Work.
Londonderry—con.	Tirkeeran,	Banagher,	Tirglassan,	1	3	16	21
	„	Clondermot,	Altnagelvin,	1	9	64	12
	„	„	Ardkill,	1	5	21	12
	„	„	Ditto,	1	4	35	25
	„	„	Drumconan,	1	4	20	12
	„	„	Lisdillon,	1	4	22	12
	„	„	Primity,	1	8	48	20
	„	„	Rossnagalliagh,	1	2	14	.
	„	Cumber, Lower,	Ardground,	1	3	16	6
	„	„	Ballymaxmore,	1	2	16	7
	„	„	Glenmadden,	1	3	21	.
	„	„	Lettermuckbury,	1	4	20	3
	„	„	Lisgrew,	1	4	25	12
	„	Cumber, Upper,	Ballyarton,	1	7	10	7
	„	„	Dungorkin,	1	4	22	10
	„	„	Killycor,	1	12	96	10
	„	„	Raspberryhill,	1	4	27	15
	„	Faughanvale,	Carnakilly, Upper,	1	4	30	4
	„	„	Derryarkin,	1	8	48	21
	„	„	Glebe,	1	4	22	.
	„	„	Ditto,	1	6	48	21
	„	„	Muff,	1	8	36	22
	„	„	Tullyverry,	1	4	24	.
	„	Learmount,	Straid,	1	5	20	20
	„	„	Tireighter,	1	6	20	.
			Total in Co. Londonderry	197	1,005	8,057	.
Monaghan,	Cremorne,	Aghnamullen,	Corduff,	1	4	20	25
	„	„	Coraness,	1	4	20	13
	„	„	Corr Hill,	1	4	14	.
	„	„	Crossreagh,	1	10	40	25
	„	„	Ditto,	1	12	20	27
	„	„	Ditto,	1	6	20	16
	„	„	Derrygooney,	1	18	20	20
	„	„	Loragh,	1	12	65	16
	„	„	Rafeeragh,	1	16	20	22
	„	„	Ditto,	1	4	20	20
	„	„	Ditto,	1	6	20	25
	„	„	Tullyglass,	1	8	50	25
	„	„	Ditto,	1	6	22	24
	„	„	Tullyrain,	1	6	20	22
	„	Ballybay,	Shantonagh,	1	4	16	27
	„	Clontibret,	Corlealackagh,	1	6	25	20
	„	„	Cremartin,	1	6	35	25
	„	„	Dernagally,	1	4	20	24
	„	„	Ditto,	1	4	22	24
	„	„	Lisgillany,	1	6	20	25
	„	„	Mey Cure,	1	4	20	15
	„	„	Ditto,	1	8	10	13
	„	„	Shancrossagh,	1	4	20	12
	„	„	Tunnagh,	1	6	20	25
	„	Muckno,	Carrickashane,	1	10	40	14
	„	„	Ditto,	1	10	40	14
	„	„	Drumleek, South,	1	12	30	14
	„	„	Ditto,	1	8	20	16
	„	„	Lurganearly,	1	6	20	20
	„	„	Lurganmore,	1	10	65	21
	„	„	Ditto,	1	8	48	21
	„	„	Tonduff,	1	4	20	24
	„	„	Tullyvaragh,	1	4	20	12
	„	Tullycorbet,	Edenmaskle,	1	4	20	21
	Dartree,	Aghabog,	Aghnameen,	1	4	22	25
	„	Clones,	Cloncore,	1	4	22	15
	„	„	Lisgilla,	1	6	20	29
	„	Currin,	Drummuckier,	1	5	20	17
	„	Ematris,	Roctor,	1	2	10	.
	Farney,	Donaghmoyne,	Aghadreenan,	1	15	60	15
	„	„	Corrintreenere,	1	1	14	18
	„	„	Donaghmoyne,	1	10	62	16
	„	„	Ditto,	1	4	20	6

RETURN of MILLS in Ireland constructed for SCUTCHING FLAX—*continued.*

PROVINCE OF ULSTER—*continued.*

County.	Barony.	Parish.	Townland.	No. of Mills.	No. of Stocks and Men Employed in each Mill: [illegible]	No. of Stocks and Men Employed in each Mill: [illegible]	No. of Weeks at Work.
Monaghan,—*contd.*	Farney,	Donaghmoyne,	Moyles,	1	8	40	9
	„	Inishkeen,	Cumliskey,	1	8	40	.
	„	„	Drumsor,	1	12	60	30
	„	Magheross,	Drummond Otra,	1	16	112	.
	„	„	Raferagh,	1	6	30	18
	„	„	Ditto,	1	6	30	78
	Monaghan,	Drumsnat,	Drumgole,	1	4	30	30
	„	Kilmore,	Drumack,	1	8	40	24
	„	„	Ditto,	1	8	56	5
	„	Monaghan,	Tonlea,	1	5	27	40
	„	„	Tullylarr,	1	3	15	.
	„	Tedavnet,	Dromgorran,	1	16	80	25
	„	„	Killyconnan,	1	6	30	4
	„	„	Quiglough,	1	6	30	8
	„	„	Terevilty,	1	6	30	.
	„	Tehallen,	Creevlea,	1	14	70	30
	„	„	Scarvagh,	1	6	30	.
	„	„	Ditto,	1	4	20	26
	„	Tullycorbet,	Corlaghurgh,	1	5	25	.
	Trough,	Donagh,	Drumcondry,	1	4	20	25
	„	„	Glasnog,	1	4	20	.
	„	„	Killicrane,	1	10	60	.
			Total in Co. Monaghan,	35	467	2,280	.
Tyrone.	Clogher,	Clogher,	Aghintain,	1	4	20	1
	„	„	Ballyvey,	1	2	10	6
	„	„	Corkhill,	1	1	4	1
	„	„	Eskragh,	1	2	10	6
	„	„	Ditto,	1	2	10	5
	„	„	Killyfaddy,	1	10	60	26
	„	„	Knockmanny,	1	6	30	30
	„	„	Tullyaloble,	1	2	10	4
	„	Donacavey,	Ardatinny,	1	2	8	.
	„	„	Ballyscanlan,	1	2	10	15
	„	„	Bleachfield,	1	10	30	16
	„	„	Garvallagh,	1	2	10	4
	„	„	Ditto,	1	10	40	16
	„	„	Lisnashillida,	1	2	18	30
	„	„	Raragh,	1	2	10	1
	„	Errigal Keerogue,	Breakagh,	1	4	24	42
	Dungannon, Lower,	Aghaloo,	Crossgail,	1	8	40	.
	„	„	Drummond,	1	8	40	46
	„	„	Ditto,	1	4	20	.
	„	„	Dyan,	1	6	30	19
	„	„	Kilmore,	1	11	70	.
	„	„	Lemnagore,	1	4	20	17
	„	„	Mullintor,	1	6	30	16
	„	„	Mulnahorn,	1	12	60	30
	„	Carnteel,	Drum,	1	4	20	.
	„	„	Lisdoart,	1	8	40	36
	„	„	Ditto,	1	18	90	15
	„	„	Ditto,	1	30	140	.
	„	Killeeshil,	Mullyroddan,	1	6	40	16
	Dungannon, Middle,	Clonfeacle,	Bracket,	1	16	80	30
	„	„	Brantry,	1	6	30	16
	„	„	Derrycreevy,	1	5	30	16
	„	„	Lisdermott,	1	7	35	7
	„	„	Ditto,	1	5	25	.
	„	„	Stangmore *Head*,	1	6	30	.
	„	„	Killyliss,	1	4	20	12
	„	Clonoe,	Annaghone,	1	6	30	16
	„	„	Mullaghmore,	1	8	48	20
	„	Donaghenry,	Bently,	1	4	20	21
	„	„	Shanley,	1	8	48	16
	„	„	Ditto,	1	4	20	20
	„	„	Stevenson's Dowery,	1	16	96	30
	„	„	Tullydg,	1	2	10	.
	„	Donaghmore,	Drumreany,	1	6	35	25
	„	„	Killymaddy,	1	6	30	12

RETURN of MILLS in Ireland constructed for SCUTCHING FLAX—continued.

PROVINCE OF ULSTER—continued.

County.	Barony.	Parish.	Townland.	No. of Mills.	No. of Stocks and Handles in each Mill: Stocks.	Handles.	No. of Weeks at Work.
Tyrone—continued.	Dungannon, Middle,	Donaghmore,	Lisnallen,	1	5	60	30
	"	"	Tullyvara,	1	6	30	30
	"	Killyman,	Coleman,	1	7	70	.
	"	"	Drumanphy,	1	4	30	.
	"	"	Drumkee,	1	12	60	.
	"	"	Dungorman,	1	6	20	30
	"	"	Mullaghbridge,	1	4	36	.
	"	"	Terduffkeel,	1	5	60	15
	"	Pomeroy,	Crossdernot,	1	4	24	17
	Dungannon, Upper,	Arboe,	Ballyneill,	1	4	24	.
	"	"	Brookend,	1	12	78	30
	"	"	Carnan,	2	4	20	.
	"	Ardtrea,	Killeenagh,	1	6	36	15
	"	"	Ditto,	1	5	36	.
	"	"	Ditto,	1	16	60	7
	"	"	Tullyreagh,	1	19	114	36
	"	Ballyclog,	Back, Lower,	1	12	60	30
	"	"	Killeenan,	1	8	12	.
	"	"	Lurk,	1	4	24	15
	"	Derryloran,	Drumgarrell,	1	8	48	.
	"	"	Feaguran,	1	4	24	20
	"	"	Gortalowry,	1	18	78	.
	"	"	Gortreagh,	1	1	24	30
	"	"	Killymoon Demesne,	1	6	36	.
	"	"	Tullywiggan,	1	6	30	15
	"	"	Ditto,	1	4	24	.
	"	"	Ditto,	1	6	30	.
	"	Desertcreat,	Dunnaforest,	1	9	45	30
	"	"	Donaghrisk,	1	6	36	32
	"	"	Gortfad,	1	4	24	30
	"	Kildress,	Cavankeeny,	1	6	36	27
	"	"	Corkhill,	1	4	24	21
	"	"	Corvanaghan,	1	6	36	17
	"	"	Kildress, Upper,	1	6	36	15
	"	"	Ditto,	1	6	36	27
	"	"	Knockaleery,	1	6	36	30
	"	"	Tamlaght,	1	5	36	19
	"	"	Tamnaskeeny,	1	10	60	.
	"	"	Ditto,	1	4	24	.
	"	"	Tulnacross,	1	6	36	18
	"	"	Ditto,	1	5	31	16
	"	Tamlaght,	Coagh,	1	6	30	30
	"	"	Ditto,	1	6	31	.
	"	"	Drummurray,	1	12	60	19
	Omagh, East,	Cappagh,	Camp,	1	6	36	.
	"	Clogherny,	Brough,	1	17	78	10
	"	"	Seskinore,	1	2	20	32
	"	Donacavey,	Tummery,	1	4	24	35
	"	Dromore,	Aghadarragh,	1	10	70	30
	"	"	Dullaghan,	1	6	30	32
	"	"	Gardrum,	1	13	78	30
	"	"	Mullaghmore,	1	8	14	4
	"	"	Raheen,	1	4	24	30
	"	"	Shanmaragh,	1	4	28	30
	"	Drumragh,	Aghnahoe,	1	1	7	.
	"	"	Blacksessiagh,	1	6	42	32
	"	"	Cloghog, Upper,	1	8	48	32
	"	"	Edergoole, Lower,	1	4	24	30
	"	"	Gillygooly,	1	4	22	10
	"	"	Ditto,	1	4	25	32
	"	"	Kilmore,	1	5	31	15
	"	"	Mullaghmore (Young),	1	7	16	.
	"	"	Tattyreel (Rogers),	1	4	22	32
	"	Kilskeery,	Moorfield,	1	4	9	.
	"	Termonmaguirk,	Aghnagreggan,	1	6	36	35
	"	"	Altanagh,	1	4	30	15
	"	"	Bracky,	1	4	30	.
	Omagh, West,	Ardstraw,	Coolaghey,	1	4	24	15
	"	"	Garvetagh, Lower,	1	3	16	8
	"	"	Gelan (Sproule),	1	4	32	35
	"	"	Spamount,	1	21	120	32
	"	Longfield, East,	Clareglmore,	1	18	78	40

RETURN of MILLS in Ireland constructed for SCUTCHING FLAX—continued.

PROVINCE OF ULSTER—continued.

County.	Barony.	Parish.	Townland.	No. of Mills.	No. of Stocks and Handles in each Mill. Stocks.	Handles.	No. of Weeks at Work.
Tyrone—continued.	Omagh, West,	Longfield, West,	Drumeevan,	1	8	14	32
	"	"	Leckagh,	1	4	32	16
	"	Termonmaguirk,	Edenreagh,	1	6	48	20
	"	"	Mourning,	1	6	64	16
	"	"	Ditto,	1	6	42	24
	"	Urney,	Churchtown,	1	12	72	6
	"	"	Garvaghan (Hemphill),	1	6	48	16
	"	"	Killeleena,	1	2	14	4
	Strabane, Lower,	Ardstraw,	Altdoghal,	1	4	28	20
	"	"	Ballyrenan,	1	4	28	4
	"	"	Bleaghe,	1	12	96	44
	"	"	Bomaly,	1	9	64	22
	"	"	Cavanderragh,	1	4	28	12
	"	"	Ditto,	1	4	28	.
	"	"	Crew, Upper,	1	6	42	20
	"	"	Derrygoon,	1	10	80	12
	"	"	Druminnagh,	1	6	48	24
	"	"	Drumlegagh,	1	4	30	4
	"	"	Ditto,	1	4	30	4
	"	"	Ditto,	1	4	28	22
	"	"	Drumnabey,	1	6	46	25
	"	"	Erganagh,	1	6	42	28
	"	"	Fyfin,	1	10	70	28
	"	"	Killeen,	1	4	28	16
	"	"	Killymore,	1	3	21	.
	"	"	Kilstrule,	1	10	76	22
	"	"	Ditto,	1	4	28	20
	"	"	Knockiniller,	1	9	61	24
	"	"	Knockroe,	1	4	32	28
	"	"	Lisnacreaght,	1	4	32	18
	"	"	Magheracolton,	1	4	32	44
	"	"	Magherakreggan,	1	4	28	20
	"	"	Milltown,	1	4	28	48
	"	"	Ditto,	1	6	42	20
	"	"	Scarvagherin,	1	10	70	16
	"	"	Ditto,	1	4	28	6
	"	"	Skinboy,	1	6	42	16
	"	Camus,	Camus,	1	4	32	18
	"	"	Carrigallen,	1	4	28	20
	"	"	Cavanalee,	1	4	28	22
	"	Donaghedy,	Altrest,	1	6	48	19
	"	"	Ditto,	1	4	30	24
	"	"	Ballyneaner,	1	2	16	15
	"	"	Ditto,	1	4	28	27
	"	"	Barnamore,	1	4	25	12
	"	"	Castlemellan,	1	4	28	20
	"	"	Dunnamanagh,	1	7	40	16
	"	"	Glenmornan and Glebe,	1	4	28	8
	"	"	Gortileck,	1	2	16	17
	"	"	Killenny,	1	6	42	18
	"	"	Ditto,	1	4	32	12
	"	"	Lisdivin, Lower,	1	4	28	23
	"	"	Milltown,	1	4	28	25
	"	"	Ditto,	1	4	28	16
	"	"	Ditto,	1	4	32	20
	"	"	Rousky,	1	4	32	12
	"	"	Sandville,	1	4	28	24
	"	"	Tullyard,	1	6	40	20
	"	Leckpatrick,	Artigarvan,	1	2	8	6
	"	"	Ballymagorry,	1	6	48	20
	"	"	Leckpatrick,	1	6	48	20
	"	"	Loughneas,	1	4	28	20
	"	"	Ditto,	1	4	24	4
	"	"	[illegible]	1	6	48	.
	"	"	Milltown,	1	8	64	20
	"	"	Tamnaparks,	1	8	64	28
	"	Urney,	Clady,	1	4	28	21
	"	"	Derrygoonan,	1	6	48	20
	"	"	Drumnagh,	1	6	48	21
	"	"	[illegible]	1	7	56	19
	"	"	Glentown,	1	6	42	16
	"	"	Ditto,	1	6	42	16

Return of Mills in Ireland constructed for Scutching Flax—continued.

PROVINCE OF ULSTER—continued.

County.	Barony.	Parish.	Townland.	No. of Mills.	No. of Stocks and Handles in each Mill. Stocks.	Handles.	No. of Weeks at Work.
Tyrone—continued.	Strabane, Lower,	Urney,	Inchenny,	1	6	46	30
	"	"	Ditto,	1	6	32	22
	"	"	Ditto,	1	3	14	2
	Strabane, Upper,	Bodoney, Lower,	Dromlee,	1	4	32	20
	"	"	Woodbrook,	1	4	38	21
	"	Bodoney, Upper,	Glenhyrgolgan,	1	4	36	23
	"	Cappagh,	Ballyreenallan,	1	1	20	22
	"	"	Bolenny,	1	4	37	6
	"	"	Dunbreen,	1	4	39	16
	"	"	Ditto,	1	4	39	20
	"	"	Killen,	1	6	42	10
	"	"	Knockanoyle,	1	5	40	16
	"	"	Malin,	1	6	30	6
	"	"	Mullaghmore,	1	5	46	18
	"	"	Ditto,	1	1	27	15
	"	"	Tullymoyle,	1	4	28	29
	"	"	Tirmoorty,	1	4	38	26
	"	"	Tirgale,	1	2	12	18
	"	"	Tully,	1	8	40	45
	"	Termonamaguirk,	Drummshilly,	1	5	36	19
			Total in Co. Tyrone,	202	1,248	7,838	.
			TOTAL IN PROVINCE OF ULSTER,	1,325	[illegible]	[illegible]	.

PROVINCE OF CONNAUGHT.

County.	Barony.	Parish.	Townland.	No. of Mills.	Stocks.	Handles.	No. of Weeks at Work.
Galway,	Ballymoe,	Drumatemple,	Ballymoe Town,	1	6	20	.
	Leitrim,	Ballynakill,	Keyaninagar,	1	1	32	.
	Moycullen,	Moycullen,	Spiddle, East,	1	2	15	25
	Tiaquin,	Boyounagh,	Boyounagh Beg,	1	6	30	28
			Total in Co. Galway,	4	19	107	.
Leitrim,	Dromahaire,	Cloonclare,	Manorhamilton,	1	3	18	.
	Leitrim,	Kiltoghert,	Carrickerry,	1	4	20	.
	Mohill,	Cloone,	Mullaghbrack,	1	6	36	.
	"	Mohill,	Roosky,	1	2	18	.
	Rosclogher,	Cloonlogher,	Cherrybrook,	1	4	20	.
	"	Rossinver,	Mullanaleck,	1	6	64	14
			Total in Co. Leitrim,	6	27	170	.
Mayo,	Carra,	Touaghty,	Cloghmoskan,	1	9	42	13
	"	"	Lecknamona,	1	8	46	13
	Gallen,	Killasser,	Ballytrasy,	1	19	60	.
	Murrisk,	Oughaval,	Baleiara,	1	4	8	.
	Tirawley,	Addergoole,	Ballyduffy,	1	6	16	10
	"	Ballysakeery,	Farragh,	1	12	32	24
	"	Doonfeeny,	Ballinglen,	1	8	60	12
	"	Kilfian,	Castlereagh,	1	8	48	.
	"	Templemurry,	Rathbawn,	1	8	40	20
			Total in Co. Mayo,	9	74	367	.
Roscommon,	Athlone,	St. Peter's,	Ballymurray,	1	2	8	.
	Ballintober, North,	Termonbarry,	Rooskey,	1	12	60	9
	Boyle,	Boyle,	Glebe,	1	10	80	20
	Roscommon,	Bumlin,	Castlecoote,	1	16	80	.
	"	Cloonfinlough,	Cloonslanor,	1	10	60	.
	"	Elphin,	Killynagh More,	1	8	48	.
			Total in Co. Roscommon,	6	58	376	.

Return of Mills in Ireland employed for Scutching Flax—continued.

PROVINCE OF CONNAUGHT—continued.

County.	Barony.	Parish.	Townland.	Number of Mills.	No. of Stocks and Handles in each Mill. Stocks.	Handles.	No. of Weeks at Work.
Sligo.	Leyny,	Achonry,	Carry,	1	12	60	3
	Tireragh,	Kilmacshalgan,	[illegible],	1	16	80	20
	"	"	Ditto,	1	16	80	20
	"	"	Ballyholan,	1	16	80	20
	Tirerril,	[illegible],	[illegible],	1	4	24	-
			Total in Co. Sligo,	5	64	324	-
			TOTAL IN PROVINCE OF CONNAUGHT,	20	243	1,244	-
			TOTAL IN IRELAND,	1,427	9,157	[illegible]	-

COPY of FORM used in collecting the Returns of Mills for Scutching Flax.

AGRICULTURAL STATISTICS, IRELAND, 1872.—FORM D.

County———— Barony———— Constabulary District———— Sub-District————

RETURN of all Scutching Mills, whether idle or at work, situated within the Enumeration District allotted to ————, showing the Power employed in each Mill, with the Names and Addresses of the Owners.

Description of Power (Steam Power, Water Power, Horse Power, Wind Power)	Total Number in each Mill. Stocks.*	Handles.*	Situation. Parish.	Townland, or Street and Town.	Owner. Name.	Address.	No. of Weeks at Work from 1st June, 1871, to 31st May, 1872.

Dated at ————, this —— day of ————, 1872.

Signature of Enumerator ————

A Return is to be forwarded for each Enumeration District.

If more than one Form is required, two or more may be attached together.

If there is not a Scutching Mill within the Enumeration District, a statement to that effect should be furnished, written on a form D.

If a Scutching Mill which was returned last year has been converted into a Mill of a different kind, or has been taken down, or has since fallen to ruin, the fact should be stated—on form D—filling up the particulars of "*Situation*" and "*Owner*."

* The STOCKS of Scutching Mills are the benches or tables on which the flax to be scutched is placed; and the HANDLES (or wipers) are the portions of the Machinery which strike the flax.

GENERAL REGISTER OFFICE,
CHARLEMONT HOUSE,
DUBLIN.

WILLIAM DONNELLY,
Registrar-General.

COPIES of the CIRCULARS and FORMS used in obtaining the average yield of the CROPS per acre, for 1873.

General Register Office,

Charlemont House, Dublin,

1st *November*, 1873.

SIR,

You will receive herewith blank copies of "Form C." referred to in the "General Instructions" addressed to the Enumerators on the 15th of May, in order to enable you to procure *Returns of the Rates of Produce* of the various Crops grown in each *Electoral Division* of your District. The Returns should be sent to this Office—*in one file*—when completed.

I beg you will be so good as to select for this service Enumerators known to you *for their intelligence and acquaintance with the parties resident in the Electoral Divisions* for which the Returns are required. Instructions as to the method of filling the Forms are printed on them. *Pray direct the Enumerators to pay particular attention to these instructions.*

From the friendly co-operation and assistance afforded to the Enumerators by all ranks and classes when collecting the Agricultural Returns for this year, I confidently trust that by making inquiries from the resident Gentry, Clergy, and intelligent Farmers in the District, a valuable approximation will be arrived at as to the average Rates of Produce per Acre of the various kinds of Grain, Potatoes, and other Crops grown in the several Electoral Divisions;—that being the object of this Return,—to which accuracy, *as far as possible*, can alone give any real value.

Your attention is particularly requested to this subject, in consequence of the increasing importance of Agricultural Statistics, and I trust you will be enabled to forward the Returns for your District to this Office on or before the 21st of November, in order that a General Abstract of the results may be compiled and submitted for the consideration of His Excellency the Lord Lieutenant.

It is my intention, in future years, to solicit the assistance of the Boards of Guardians on this difficult question, in order that I may have the advantage of their opinions as to the average Rates of Produce in the several Electoral Divisions. This information will form a valuable auxiliary to that obtained through the Constabulary.

I am, Sir,

Your faithful servant,

WILLIAM DONNELLY,

Registrar-General.

To the Sub-Inspector,

Royal Irish Constabulary.

AGRICULTURAL STATISTICS—IRELAND, 1873.—FORM C.

County of ———— Union of ————

Constabulary District of ———— Electoral Division of ————

RETURN showing the Estimated Average Produce per English and Irish Acre, of the following Crops in the Electoral Division of ————.

Crops.	Produce of the Electoral Division. Per English or Statute Acre.	Per Irish Acre.	[illegible]
Wheat, in cwts. of 112 lbs.			
Oats, [illegible]			
Barley, [illegible]			
Bere, [illegible]			
Rye, [illegible]			
Beans, [illegible]			
Peas, [illegible]			
Potatoes, [illegible]			
Turnips, in tons			
Mangel Wurzel, [illegible]			
Carrots, [illegible]			
Cabbage, [illegible]			
Green Fodder (*for feeding purposes*), in tons			
Flax, [illegible]			
Rape (*for feeding purposes*), in tons			
Hay, in tons			

* NOTE.—[illegible]

I certify that I have obtained the information embodied in the foregoing Return from the Persons above named, who in my opinion were well qualified to give it, and I believe the Estimated Average Rates of Produce to be correct. Dated at ———— this —— day of ——, 1873.

(*Signature of the Enumerator*)————

I believe the foregoing Return to be correct.

———— *Sub-Inspector.*

INSTRUCTIONS.

1. In filling in the Rate of Produce, the yield will be stated per Irish and also per *English or Statute Acre*, for each Crop, and the *Enumerator will be careful to enter the Rate in the Weights* (Act 22 and 23 Vic., cap. 72.) mentioned opposite to the respective Crops named on the other side of this Form. It is particularly to be borne in mind that the average *yield per Acre* is for the *entire* Electoral Division—not for any individual Farm or portion of the Electoral Division.

2. One Form will be filled by the Enumerator for each *Electoral Division* which is altogether within the Constabulary District; for such Electoral Divisions as are in two or more Constabulary Districts, the Sub-Inspectors will arrange on which District the duty will devolve of obtaining the information, as it is very desirable that only *one* Form C be forwarded for each Electoral Division.

3. The information as to the probable yield of the Electoral Division for which the Return is made, should be obtained from intelligent Landholders of the District, whose Names and Addresses will be entered in the column left for that purpose.

4. The greatest care should be taken in filling these Forms, and the information should be obtained and the Return sent to the Sub-Inspector of the District, on the 10th of November—sooner if practicable.

5. In those parts of the country in which the Cunningham Measure is used, the word "*Irish*" may be erased with the pen, and the word "Cunningham" substituted at the head of the column. The Enumerator is requested to reduce *Irish*, or Cunningham measure, by the Form supplied for that purpose, viz., Form H, which gives to the nearest quarter the equivalent English or *Statute Measure*; and no fractions less than one-quarter should be used in either the English or Irish terms.

WILLIAM DONNELLY, *Registrar-General.*

General Register Office,

Charlemont House, Dublin,

November, 1873.

General Register Office,
Charlemont House, Dublin.

GENTLEMEN, *December*, 1878.

I beg to enclose copies of Returns showing the estimated average produce, by the *English* and also by the *Irish Acre*, of the various crops grown in 1878 within each Electoral Division of your Union, in order to obtain from the Guardians their opinion as to whether the AVERAGE PRODUCE per ACRE—obtained by the Enumerators from practical Landholders,—fairly represents the yield of the respective crops.

In case the Guardians consider the Returns any rate, entered upon it to be above or below what it should be, columns are provided in which to insert the corrected rate.

As these Forms may be filled without imposing much trouble, I shall feel obliged if the Guardians will be so good as to favour me with their opinion respecting the produce of the various crops grown this year in their Union, and thus aid in increasing the value of these Returns, which are of so much general importance to the community.

May I request you will be so good as to give directions to the Clerk of your Board to return these *Forms* to me as soon as possible, as they are required to assist in compiling for publication the Table of *corrected* average produce of the Crops in 1878.

In case it is found inconvenient to obtain the signature of an Ex-Officio or Elected Guardian particularly connected with any Electoral Division, the signature of any other Guardian acquainted with the District will be sufficient, or, if these average rates of produce are discussed and decided upon at a Meeting of the Board, the signature of the Chairman, or of the Clerk, if authorized, will answer the purpose.

I take this opportunity of expressing my obligations to the many Guardians who have been so kind as to assist me in the revision of the Returns of the average produce in former years, and I trust that, on public grounds, I may be excused for soliciting the opinion of your Board on this subject.

Communications to this Office need not be prepaid.

I am, Gentlemen, your faithful servant,

WILLIAM DONNELLY, *Registrar-General.*

To the Chairman and Board of Guardians

AGRICULTURAL STATISTICS—IRELAND, 1878.

RATES OF PRODUCE.

Union of ——— Electoral Division of ———

AVERAGE RATES of PRODUCE for the undermentioned Crops, as made by the Constabulary Enumerators, submitted *for the opinion of the Guardians.*

Crops.	Average Produce as returned by the Constabulary Enumerators. Per Statute or English Acre.	Per Irish Acre.	Corrected Average Produce according to the opinion of the Guardians. Per Statute or English Acre.	Per Irish Acre.
Wheat, in barrels of 112 lbs. [illegible]				
[illegible]				
Hay, in tons,				

In my opinion, the Average Rates of Produce returned by the Constabulary Enumerators for the above Electoral Division are fairly stated, except for those Crops opposite to which an amended Rate is given.

Signature of Guardian ——— *Date* ———

The Registrar-General requests that the Guardian to whom this Form is forwarded for revision will be so good as to return it to the Clerk of the Union, signed and dated, at his EARLIEST convenience, for transmission to the GENERAL REGISTER OFFICE, CHARLEMONT HOUSE, DUBLIN.

EMIGRATION

COPY of the FORM used in taking an Account of the Emigrants from the different Ports of Ireland.

EMIGRANT RETURN. EMIGRATION FROM IRELAND, 1878.

County of ——— *Constabulary District of* ——— *Port of* ———

RETURN of all Emigrants and Passengers who left this Port on board the ———, bound for ———, on the —— day of ———, 1878.

In filling this Return observe the Instructions for Enumerators of Emigration, on Circular No. [illegible]

No.	Names of Emigrants and Passengers. Christian Names.	Surnames.	Age. Years, [illegible]	Months, [illegible]	Sex. M.	F.	[illegible] "Em."	"Pas."	Rank, Profession, or Occupation. [illegible]	[illegible] From what County.	[illegible]
1											
2											
3											
4											
5											
6											
7											
8											
9											
10											

APPROVED.
[illegible],
[illegible].

WILLIAM DONNELLY,
Registrar-General.

I certify that the above is a correct Return.
Dated at ———, *the* —— *day of* ———, 1878.
Signature and Rank of Enumerator ———

www.ingramcontent.com/pod-product-compliance
Lightning Source LLC
Chambersburg PA
CBHW021644270326
41931CB00008B/1157
* 9 7 8 3 7 4 1 1 2 2 1 9 4 *